MYSTERIES
OF THE ANCIENT WORLD

MYSTERIES
OF THE ANCIENT WORLD

EDITOR: JUDITH FLANDERS

BARNES
&NOBLE
BOOKS
NEW YORK

This edition published by
Barnes & Noble, Inc.,
by arrangement with
The Orion Publishing Group Ltd
1998 Barnes & Noble Books

First published in one volume in Great Britain in 1998
by Weidenfeld & Nicolson

M 10 9 8 7 6 5 4 3 2 1
ISBN 0-7607-1134-8

Jacket design: Michelle MacCreadie
Text design: Kate Shackleford
Typeset in Baskerville

WEIDENFELD & NICOLSON
The Orion Publishing Group Ltd
Orion House
5 Upper Saint Martin's Lane
London WC2H 9EA

CONTENTS

IN THE BEGINNING

THE ARCHAEOLOGICAL EVIDENCE

MYTHS & LEGENDS?

IN THE
BEGINNING

THE EXTINCTION OF THE DINOSAURS

THE LAST NEANDERTHALS

THE EXTINCTION OF THE
DINOSAURS

DOUGLAS PALMER

First meat-eater: a jawbone from Oxford with flesh-cutting teeth was given the name Megalosaurus *(meaning giant lizard) in 1822.*

The word 'dinosaur' has something of a double meaning, there is the metaphorical dinosaur, the 'has been' . . . 'consigned to the dustbin of history' and then there are the 'dinosaurs' of Jurassic Park, *beloved by children of all ages.*

These dinosaurs are either seemingly benign plant-eaters, or 'bad guys', red-eyed, ravenous meat-eating predators. Why, of all the groups of animals and plants that have become extinct over the last 600 million years and more of life on earth, should the dinosaurs have acquired this image? Part of the explanation is that when the dinosaurs were invented in the nineteenth century, they inherited

the mantle of the dragons of myth and folklore. Since then the image of the dinosaurs has gone through a number of transformations which have kept them in fashion.

The remains of these mysterious animals combine immensity of size with the curiously inexpressive, staring creepiness of reptiles. How much truth is there behind this image? What were these dinosaurs really like? Does their rise and fall justify their status as an object lesson in why not to overdo things and become a victim of your own success?

In late Permian times, some 230 million years before humans appeared on Earth, a group of scaly-skinned, egg-laying reptiles evolved and gradually came to dominate the planet. For over 155 million years, these now-extinct reptiles, which came to be known as dinosaurs, ruled the landscapes of the world from Alaska to Antarctica. In the history of life, no other group of animals has been so successful for so long. So far, mammals have only been in charge for a mere 65 million years. One of the great mysteries of the dinosaurs is why, if they were so

Puzzling bones: in the 1820s Doctor Gideon Mantell struggled to identify fossil bones from a quarry in Sussex.

9

Under Richard Owen's instruction, Waterhouse Hawkins drew and modelled the first dinosaurs as heavyweight rhinoceros-like lizards.

successful, did they die out 65 million years ago? Why should the dinosaurs have been 'deselected', while other reptiles, such as terrestrial crocodiles and lizards and aquatic turtles, survived and prospered? Did they fall because they were unable to adapt and change, or were they blasted off by a meteorite? Did it all end with a whimper or a bang?

Until the end of the eighteenth century the Old Testament view of creation was the prevailing one, and the world was believed to be 6,000 years old. The history and evolution of life on earth that is accepted today was not discovered until the nineteenth century, and one of the greatest and most surprising scientific discoveries of nineteenth-century science was that of the extinct fossil reptiles, especially the dinosaurs.

The First Discoveries

Before the dinosaurs were 'invented' the first intimation that the world had once been populated by weird and wonderful animals that no longer existed was provided by the discovery in 1786 of an enormous skull with metre-long jaws, armed with ferocious teeth in a chalk quarry in Maastricht, Netherlands. Scientists could not agree on what kind of animal it had been, for it looked like a cross between a crocodile and toothed whale, so it was reconstructed as a crocodile-like animal. Although no such animal was known at the time, it was still possible that such an animal might exist somewhere on earth: extinction had not yet been thought of. Such was the Beast of Maastricht's fame that, in 1795, it was captured by Napoleon's army and exhibited in Paris.

Some of the most important early finds of ancient monsters were made at the very beginning of the nineteenth century. They were found by a Dorset woman, Mary Anning, and her family in the 200-million-year-old rocks of Lyme Regis on the south coast of England. The family eked out a precarious existence scouring the limestone cliffs for fossils to sell to growing numbers of tourists who came to admire the wild seascape and its 'quaint native' inhabitants.

Between 1811 and 1830 the Annings uncovered complete flattened skeletons of creatures up to 4 metres long, which had toothed beaks like mammalian dolphins mixed with other, predominantly reptilian characteristics. These ichthyosaurs (meaning fish-lizards) and plesiosaurs (near-lizards) had evidently lived in ancient seas, because they were found with the shells of typically marine clams, starfish and squid-like cephalopods. The likelihood of extinction was becoming more acceptable, but the question of how and when it occurred was still highly contentious. After all, as recorded in the Bible, the Flood could well have been responsible for drowning all these fossil creatures found in the rocks.

Eminent scientists of the day visited the Annings' little fossil shop and bought specimens for the growing collections of the university museums of Cambridge and Oxford and the national collection in London. They were the first 'fossil dragons' to stir the public imagination – even the King of Saxony visited Mary to admire the results of her labours – and the first large extinct animals to be illustrated in reconstructions of their living environments. These early-Victorian illustrations provided the model for today's cryptic beasts, such as the Loch Ness 'monster'.

In 1825 some mysterious fossil bones were found near Cuckfield, Sussex. The fossils included a few peculiar leaf-shaped teeth with serrated edges and a jumble of bones, including a single conical spike or horn-shaped bone about 15 centimetres long. The local doctor and naturalist, Gideon Mantell, was puzzled. However, it was clear that here were the remains of a land-living reptile of several metres size.

The only models scientists had to go on were the living four-legged reptiles – the lizards and crocodiles. Mantell's reconstruction of the animal seems to owe as much to the myth and imagery of St George, and was a distinctly dragon-like beast, with legs sticking out on either side, rather than tucked in below the bulk of the body as seen in mammals. He placed the spike, rhinoceros-like, on the end of its nose.

Inventing Dinosaurs

Dinosaurs were not 'invented' until 1842, when a British scientist, Richard Owen, first coined the name 'Dinosauria', meaning 'terrible lizard', to distinguish the recently named fossil reptiles *Iguanodon*, *Hylaeosaurus* and *Megalosaurus* from the known living reptiles. Owen calculated that his dinosaurs might be as much as six times the size of an elephant, but that was before 'dinoflation' set in. Little did he know at the time exactly what sort of monster he was creating. His creation was to become a universal icon, eclipsing dragons and even outshining Mary Shelley's monstrous Frankenstein.

The relocation of Joseph Paxton's Crystal Palace from Kensington to Sydenham gave Owen a golden opportunity to recreate his concept of the dinosaur in the form of life-size models set in appropriate landscape and vegetation. Owen supervised the modelling by Benjamin Waterhouse Hawkins, and the opening by Queen Victoria drew crowds of thousands. The first theme park in the world was open.

News of the venture soon spread and Hawkins

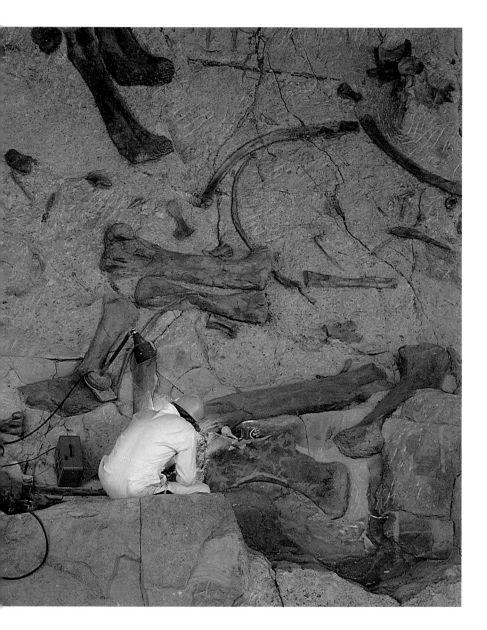

Dinosaur graveyard: the discovery in America of abundant dinosaur fossils in the late nineteenth century revolutionized ideas on how they looked.

prints while ploughing on the family farm in Massachusetts. A local naturalist, Edward Hitchcock, eventually described the prints in 1836, and went on to make an impressive collection of other fossil tracks from the red sandstones of Connecticut.

The distinctive and puzzling feature of the tracks was that they had been made by large two-legged animals with three toes on each foot. At the time, the only creatures known to produce such tracks were birds, so not unreasonably Hitchcock concluded that they must have been made by giant birds. But what he had found were actually bipedal dinosaur footprints and so these fossil tracks provided the first evidence that not all dinosaurs were four-legged, as everyone had assumed.

The study of fossil tracks has really taken off in recent years, with amazing finds ranging from the enormous prints of individual sauropods to multiple trackways showing that many dinosaurs were social animals. The plant-eaters formed herds for mutual protection, just as elephants do today, and some of the small carnivores probably hunted in packs or family groups, like lions and hyenas.

In 1858, Joseph Leidy found a partial skeleton in New Jersey, which he reconstructed in a two-legged kangaroo-like posture; but the hunt moved west and really began to take off in the 1870s. Two schoolmasters, Arthur Lakes and O. W. Lucas, independently found dinosaur fossils in Colorado and sent their finds to experts back east.

The first intimation that the hunters were on to something big came in the 1880s when Othneil Marsh of Yale produced the first reconstruction of a sauropod, which he called *Brontosaurus*, meaning 'thunder lizard'. Marsh was somewhat cavalier when he first cobbled together his *Brontosaurus* reconstruction in 1883, for it included the limb-bones and skull of *Camarasaurus*, a quite different animal, and scientists no longer use the name *Brontosaurus*.

With individual limb-bones over a metre long and what seemed like endless vertebrae, it was clear that once upon a time there had been dinosaurs that were by far the largest animals to have lived on land. The unforgettable image of giant plant-eating sauropods over 20 metres long and weighing more than 20 tonnes, supported by elephantine pillar-like legs, had invaded the public conscience. Indeed, the bulk of these creatures was

was invited to repeat his success in New York's Central Park. He set about producing an even more ambitious scheme with many more reconstructions. Unfortunately, the scheme fell foul of local politics and failed but some of the completed models are reputed to have been broken up and buried in the park (despite searches no remains have been discovered). However, the impetus for dinosaur research had taken off in America in a big way and the whole concept of the dinosaur was to change radically.

The new American image owed its birth to a discovery in 1802, when an observant youth by the name of Pliny Moody uncovered some fossil foot-

The metre-long skull of the predator Allosaurus *was reduced to a bony scaffold for strength and lightness.*

so great that it was thought they must have been primarily water-dwellers like the hippopotamus.

These dinosaur giants were so impressive that their remains were sought the world over. One of the finest discoveries was the 1907 find of a 22-metre-long *Brachiosaurus* in East Africa. Its nostrils were right on top of its head, which seemed to support the idea that these giants were aquatic. Now it is realized that *Brachiosaurus* was in fact giraffe-like in its habits and, like the other sauropods, browsed on tree and shrub foliage.

The first indication that the dinosaurs included animals that were not just big but awesomely dangerous came in 1908. An expedition from the American Museum of Natural History in New York found a skeleton of a completely new kind of dinosaur in the late Cretaceous rocks of northern Montana.

Of all the dinosaurs to have captured the public imagination, the new beast, the giant bipedal car-

nivore *Tyrannosaurus rex*, has come to epitomize all that is mean and nasty in 'dino-lore'. Standing some 14 metres high and weighing around 6 tonnes, with a fine set of 20-centimetre-long carving knives in its jaws, *T. rex* was something special. No modern land-living carnivore comes anywhere near this size. The teeth are designed for one thing only – meat eating. The mystery of *T. rex* relates to the question of whether it could have been an active hunter that ran down, seized and killed its own prey, as it is generally portrayed as doing.

The problem is that *T. rex* had extraordinarily small arms, which could not have played any role in capturing or holding prey. Furthermore, calculations show that a beast this size and weight could not have run any faster than about 12 kilometres per hour. If *T. rex* tripped, its arms would not have been able to break the fall and the force of impact would have broken its massive skull. So, it is more likely that they were scavengers, seeking out kills made by other smaller and more active carnivorous dinosaurs.

There is a considerable mystery about dinosaur reproduction and growth. Like most reptiles dinosaurs laid eggs; the question is, how big would the egg of a 50-tonne, 30-metre-long dinosaur have been? Using birds as a model and scaling up from a chicken to an ostrich and on to a large dinosaur produces the absurdity of a dinosaur egg the size and weight of a small car. Living reptiles, however, such as large crocodiles, which can weigh up to one tonne, lay eggs about the size of a billiard ball, which is relatively small in relation to their body weight. On this scale, the egg of a 50-tonne dinosaur would still be about 20 kilograms. So far, the largest dinosaur eggs to be found have a weight of no more than 6 kilograms but are remarkably elongated. A baby curled inside such an egg, would be over a metre in length on hatching, which is still very small compared with its 30-metre mother. With such a size discrepancy, it is unlikely that its mother could look after the baby and its numerous siblings. These babies must have been capable of fending for themselves almost as soon as they were hatched, just as turtles are.

However, smaller dinosaurs probably had other breeding strategies that required more parental care. Since 1922 and the first discovery of dinosaur nests and eggs in Mongolia it has been evident that at least some dinosaurs lived in social groups and may have cared for their young just as crocodiles do today.

Dino Demise

The mystery of the disappearance of the dinosaurs has taxed scientists for many years now and hundreds of different theories have been put forward to explain what happened to them. Most of these ideas range from the ridiculous to the unlikely, and include death by viral infection, food poisoning, laying eggs with shells too thick for the babies to break out of and producing progeny of only one sex. Yet some of these theories are not as crazy as they might at first seem. It is known that the sex of crocodile hatchlings is partly determined by the temperature at which they incubate in the nest; global climate change might have done the same for the dinosaurs. Of one thing there is no doubt, the scaly-skinned dinosaurs did die out some 65

King of the Beasts. The popular image of the dinosaurs was transformed by the discovery of the giant carnivore Tyrannosaurus rex.

million years ago. However, their end is not conveniently marked in the rocks by a global fossil graveyard, stacked full of bones, with dated headstones.

One of the problems is that there are not enough dinosaur fossils to test an enforced extinction theory against that of gradual decline and disappearance. By late Cretaceous times there were only about fifty kinds of dinosaurs left. By comparison, sea life was much more abundant, with many fossils to be found in the marine rock record. Here, the change from Cretaceous to Tertiary times, which coincides with the extinction event, is well marked by a thin layer of sediment. The layer contains good evidence of a meteorite impact; there is a chemical signature and tiny glass beads of fused rock, which were blown into the atmosphere.

A major meteorite impact should leave a distinctly large crater. After much searching, an appropriately large crater, about 100 kilometres wide, has now been found at Chicxulub, in the Yucatan peninsula, Mexico, and it seems to be about the right age. Scientists are working to date the impact as accurately as possible. They imagine that the impact threw so much dust into the atmosphere that global temperatures dropped far enough seriously to disturb ecosystems at sea and on land. It follows that any related extinction should be post-impact.

The marine fossil evidence provides the best timing of the event and measure of its impact. Some common fossil micro-organisms suffered a 70 per cent loss of species, but the detailed distribution across the boundary shows that their decline began before the meteorite impact and continued after it. The rocks also show that there was a global fall in sea level and change in ocean circulation patterns at this time. Such changes might not have quite the same media appeal as a meteorite impact, but they are known to have a dramatic effect on life. Around 250 million years ago another even bigger environmental change wiped out 65 per cent of all life forms on earth without the assistance of any extraterrestrial bodies.

There undoubtedly was a major impact event. The scaly-skinned dinosaurs and their distant marine and flying reptilian relatives did die out, but the last known occurrences of their fossils seem to show that extinction started before the impact. At the moment, the balance of evidence indicates

that a meteorite applied the final *coup de grace* to an already declining group of animals caught up in a global phase of environmental change that originated in the oceans.

Dinosaurs Take Off?

It might seem that our metaphor is accurate, and that the dinosaurs became a 'bunch of old fossils' consigned to the dustbin of prehistory, but that is not altogether accurate because the dinosaurs have not entirely gone. In one sense they are still very much with us, it is just that they are now covered in feathers and we call them birds. But it was not a simple matter of the dinosaurs handing over the baton just as they crossed the line in the great evolutionary relay race.

The oldest fossil bird, *Archaeopteryx*, evolved some 150 million years ago. Its skeleton clearly relates the bird to the dinosaurs. The dinosaurs had taken off. It could be argued that the avian dinosaurs are even more successful than their extinct cousins. After all, with around 9,000 different species today, the birds are more successful than mammals, of which there are only some 4,000 species.

Archaeopteryx has a skeleton remarkably similar to a group of small bipedal dinosaurs called the theropods; it is quite possible that feathers evolved from reptilian scales, because they are made of similar biological ingredients. One big difference between birds and reptiles is that birds are warm-blooded. If birds evolved from dinosaurs, does this mean that dinosaurs were warm-blooded as well? And, if so, were they all warm-blooded? And anyway how could we tell from the fossils? Major questions like this remain to be answered and are part of the 'life-blood' of dinosaur studies and the continuing fascination of dinosaurs.

Understanding the cause of the extinction of the dinosaurs is not just a matter of scientific curiosity. The fossil remains of past life tell us that the history of life on earth has been full of such dramatic changes of fortune. Whole groups of organisms have come and gone through natural causes completely beyond their control. The geological record shows that climate has always changed and that humans will have to adapt to future change in order to survive. The more that is known about how extinctions happen the better – unless we want to follow the dinosaurs into oblivion.

Maiasaur (good mother lizard) nests and eggs show that some dinosaurs looked after their young like most birds do.

THE LAST
NEANDERTHALS

JOHN F. HOFFECKER

The Neanderthals are one of the great mysteries of the human past. After almost a century and a half of discovery, analysis and debate, they remain an enigma. They are very close to us in many respects, but yet very distant.

The first remains of a Neanderthal to be recognized as an early form of human were discovered in 1856 in a cave in the Neander Valley in Germany.

The Neanderthals are the last of our fossil ancestors to walk the earth, and are probably not true ancestors but actually evolutionary cousins who shared the planet with modern humans for more than 100,000 years. They seem to have been an alternative form of humankind – a variant of ourselves who possessed most of our traits but differed from us in some significant ways. Less than 30,000 years ago they vanished rather suddenly, and under suspicious circumstances.

Neanderthal Origins

In order to understand how the Neanderthals fit into the story of human evolution, we must travel back to between 6 and 10 million years ago. It is at this time that the earliest forms of humans (australopithecines) emerged in Africa, apparently in response to the shrinkage of tropical forests and corresponding growth of open landscapes. The earliest humans developed a trait that set them apart not only from their ancestral apes, but from most other mammals: the ability to walk upright on two legs. It is still not clear what advantage(s) upright locomotion conferred on the australopithecines, but by freeing the forelimbs for the making and using of tools, it set the stage for the next critical evolutionary step.

Slightly more than 2 million years ago the earliest members of the genus *Homo* appeared; they were the first humans to exhibit a pronounced increase in brain size and the first to manufacture stone tools. Once again, the causes of these developments remain unclear, but their consequences were dra-

matic; within a relatively brief period of time, the toolmakers had expanded out of Africa across the southern half of Eurasia. Early *Homo* remains from Indonesia and southern China have recently been dated to between 1.7 and 2 million years ago.

By one million years ago populations of *Homo* had begun to move northward into cooler landscapes, as revealed by recent discoveries from Spain and the southern slope of the Caucasus Mountains. These were the first early humans to invade regions as far north as the city of Madrid (40° North); by half a million years ago, they had reached central Europe (50° North). As in the case of the expansion across southern Eurasia, the invasion of northern landscapes is associated with evolutionary change. During this period we see the further increases in brain size that mark the gradual emergence of our own species *Homo sapiens*. It is from these archaic forms of *Homo sapiens* that both the Neanderthals and ourselves (*Homo sapiens sapiens*) evolved.

The first human populations to spread into northern Eurasia faced several new challenges to survival that seem to have been overcome through various behavioural and technological means (which may be related to the increases in brain size). Unfortunately,

human skeletal remains and archaeological sites from this time range are rare, and there is limited information available for reconstructing their way of life. Control of fire was probably essential for coping with the colder temperatures of northern latitudes, and the oldest convincing traces of hearths have been found at sites in north China and central Europe dated to 500,000–350,000 years ago. The reduced abundance of edible plant foods must have required a greater reliance on animal foods, although microscopic analysis of teeth in a 500,000-year-old jaw from Germany revealed the severe wear of heavy plant food consumption. Evidence of big game hunting is scarce; most meat may have been scavenged from carcasses scattered across the landscape.

Within this broader picture of northern adaptation the Neanderthals emerged as a distinct human form roughly 200,000 years ago in Europe. As in the case of the appearance of the earliest *Homo sapiens*, the transition was a gradual one, and many of the characteristic Neanderthal traits evolved over a long period of time. The Neanderthals (who are classified scientifically as *Homo sapiens neanderthalensis*) represented a significant advance over their predecessors in their ability to cope with

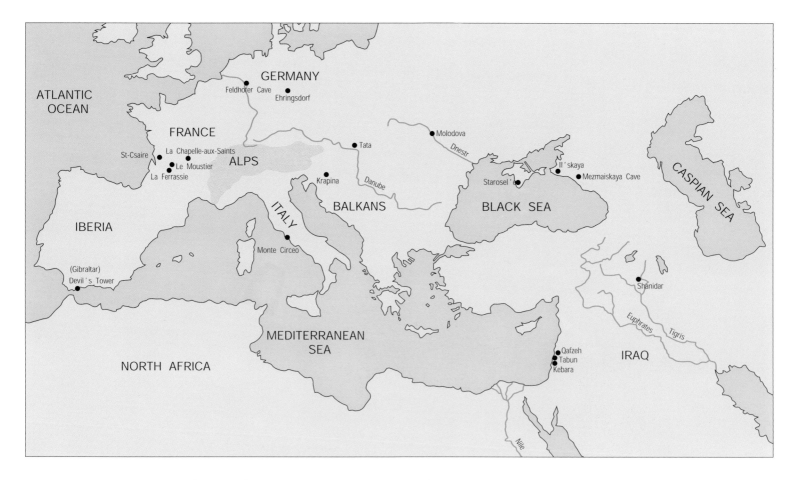

GERMANY
Feldhofer Cave
Ehringsdorf

ATLANTIC
OCEAN

FRANCE
St-Csaire
La Chapelle-aux-Saints
Le Moustier
La Ferrassie
ALPS

Molodova
Dnestr

Tata

IBERIA

ITALY

Krapina

Danube

BALKANS

Il'skaya
Starosel' \o
Mezmaiskaya Cave

BLACK SEA

CASPIAN SEA

Monte Circeo

(Gibraltar)
Devil's Tower

MEDITERRANEAN
SEA

NORTH AFRICA

Shanidar

Qafzeh
Tabun
Kebara

IRAQ

Euphrates
Tigris

Nile

northern environments. This is strikingly evident in the distribution of their remains in space and time. The Neanderthals were the first humans to occupy Europe during periods of intense glacial cold; earlier human populations seemed to have abandoned higher latitudes during glacial periods. They were also the first humans to colonize the drier and colder landscapes of eastern Europe. In fact, many anthropologists have suggested that the distinctive features of Neanderthals – such as their short limbs and barrel-shaped chests – evolved as special adaptations to the cold, although it is now clear that they were present during warm periods as well. The feature that was probably most important in their conquest of new environments was their enlarged brain, which gave them the insight and imagination to devise new means of coping with the challenges of these environments.

Ironically, the origins of our own immediate ancestors (early *Homo sapiens sapiens*) remain less clear than those of our Neanderthal cousins. The lineages appear to have split at some point before 200,000 years ago, and the two forms of humankind shared the planet until roughly 30,000 years ago, when the Neanderthals vanished. While the Neanderthals occupied Europe throughout this period, our own ancestors resided in Africa. The Near East became a 'crossroads' inhabited at various times by both groups, although it is not certain that the two populations ever actually co-existed together for any length of time.

Anatomy of a Neanderthal: Brains and Muscle

Unlike earlier human forms, the Neanderthals are represented by a relative abundance of skeletal remains. This is chiefly a function of their comparatively recent age; erosion and weathering destroy most remains and the sites that contain them – including caves – in a few hundred thousand years. Anthropologists have thus acquired a wealth of bones and teeth, which they have subjected to exhaustive studies. As a result, we know a great deal about the anatomy and appearance of our late cousins, who possessed a remarkable combination of brains and muscle.

We know that the Neanderthals were highly robust and muscular, a trait that they shared with their more primitive predecessors. They were not especially tall (adult males seem to have averaged about 1.60 metres in height), but they possessed large joints, thick leg-bones, and many parts of the

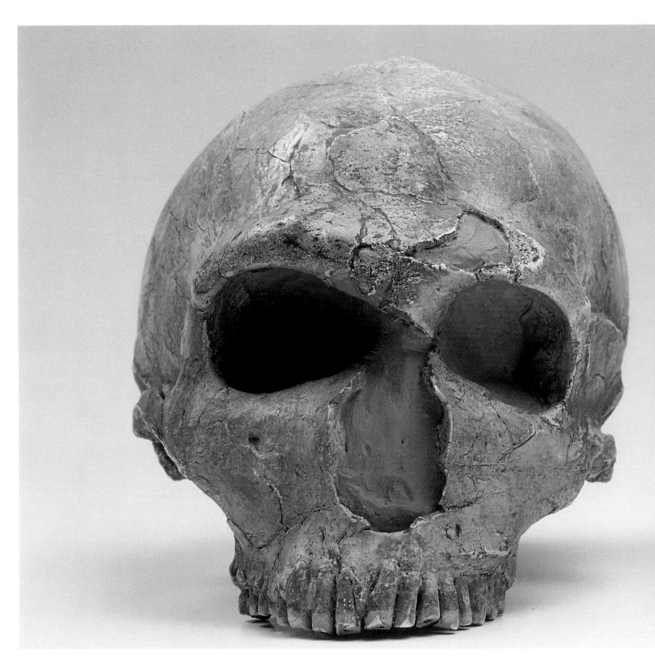

A comparison of the skull of a Neanderthal (far right) with a modern human (right) reveals the peculiar features of the former.

skeleton exhibit the deep marks of powerful muscle attachments. The bones of their children show that the robust skeleton began to develop at an early age, apparently to endure a life of heavy physical demands; most adult skeletons also reveal signs of disease and injury.

The head that rested on this muscular frame was even more striking in contrast to ourselves, and unique among human forms. The heavy brow-ridges and flattened top were also traits inherited from their predecessors, and ones that have contributed significantly to their primitive and brutish image. But the Neanderthals combined these traits with an exceptionally large brain that exceeds even our own in total volume. While modern human

brains average roughly 1,400 cubic centimetres, our sample of fossil Neanderthal skulls indicates an average brain volume of over 1,500 cubic centimetres! The elongated shape of these skulls has encouraged past speculation that the Neanderthal brain was organized differently from our own, and without comparable development of areas of higher thought. Today most anthropologists recognize that there is an insufficient basis for such conclusions, and that we must turn to other sources of information for an understanding of the Neanderthal mind.

The Neanderthal face also reflected some unique features that must have appeared odd, perhaps repulsive, to the modern humans who eventu-

ally met up with them. It possessed inflated cheeks and a remarkably prominent nose, but lacked a chin. The front teeth were excessively large and, along with the cheek teeth, were placed so far forward relative to the rest of the face that a gap existed between the last molar and the back of the jaw. Studies of the teeth reveal extreme wear, including microscopic scratches that seem to have been caused by the regular practice of cutting of materials such as animal hide held firmly in the grip of the jaw.

The Economic and Social Order

Evidence that Neanderthal daily life may have been more stressful and dangerous than that of

their modern human contemporaries leads us to wonder how much it differed from the latter. Did the Neanderthals rely more heavily on brute strength and endurance than on careful planning and technology? Anthropologists are sharply divided over this issue, either believing that the Neanderthal economy was fundamentally different from that of the modern human populations who succeeded them, or that it was quite similar.

Like all peoples of the Ice Age (and some of the post-Ice Age), the Neanderthals did not practise agriculture, but pursued an economy based on nomadic foraging. Some anthropologists have suggested that the Neanderthals lacked the advance planning and scheduling of modern human

This skeleton from Kebara Cave in Israel revealed new information about the anatomy of the Neanderthals.

foraging people, and that they wandered from place to place, often depending on chance encounters with animal prey and other sources of food. However, the study of artefacts and animal bones from the sites that they occupied reveals a pattern fundamentally similar to that of modern foragers. For example, on the slopes of the northern Caucasus Mountains in Russia, we find a diverse array of sites at varying elevations used for different purposes during different seasons of the year. The Neanderthals seemed to have visited these locations at specific times to procure locally and seasonally available foods, which must have required planned and scheduled movements and activities. There is reason to believe, however, that they moved around within smaller territories than their modern successors.

Some anthropologists have also suggested that the Neanderthals were less competent and effective hunters than modern humans. The settlement of northern environments poor in edible plant foods would have demanded a heavy reliance on animal foods, but these might have been obtained from the scavenging of carcasses rather than hunting live prey. There are sites in central Italy that appear to reflect at least partial reliance on scavenging deer carcasses. On the other hand, sites in France, Russia and elsewhere contain strong evidence for the hunting of medium and large mammals such as red deer and bison, the bones of which exhibit the marks of butchering by stone tools and lack the characteristics of the remains of animals that have succumbed to disease or non-human predators. Some Neanderthal sites even contain large quantities of the remains of herd mammals that might have been driven into ravines

or over cliffs in the manner of an Indian bison hunt on the plains of North America.

The question of Neanderthal economy is inextricably linked to that of their society. The highly flexible social organization of modern human foragers – as revealed by studies of hunting and gathering peoples like the south African Bushmen and the Eskimo – allows response to variations in the timing and location of available food sources. Thus, a small group of adult males might be despatched to the mountains for a protracted winter hunt, while a large group of males, females and children might be assembled temporarily on the plains to provide the necessary numbers for a bison herd drive in the late summer. Did Neanderthal society possess this organizational flexibility?

Once again, some anthropologists have argued that there were radical differences between the Neanderthals and modern humans. It has long been suggested that the Neanderthals lacked an incest taboo – universal among all modern human societies as far as we know – and did not follow an established pattern of mating and marriage between nuclear families (exogamy). Exogamy ensures a network of co-operative alliances among family groups that provides the foundation for modern human society, and seems to be an important part of the organizational flexibility of modern human foraging peoples. But anthropologists have found it difficult, if not impossible, to reconstruct Neanderthal society from the limited variety of remains that are available for study. To shed any light on this issue, we must turn to another aspect of Neanderthal life, and one that reveals the most dramatic and important contrast between that life and our own.

Kebara Cave in Israel was probably visited by Neanderthals about 60,000 years ago.

Language and Culture?

The critical factor in the shaping of our economic and social order is language and the use of symbols. The intricate network of alliances among families and the complex economic strategies of modern human foragers rest on language and culture – on our ability to formulate and communicate abstract concepts and shared beliefs through symbols. The development of the capacity for using symbols was the last and most significant event in the evolution of modern humans, and in the millennia following the Ice Age, as many populations began to settle down to an agricultural way of life, it provided the basis for civilization.

Despite their large brains and impressive foraging skills, there is much evidence that the Neanderthals led an existence that was largely if not wholly devoid of symbols. While the modern humans who succeeded them in Europe 30,000 years ago left behind a rich legacy of ornament and art (including spectacular paintings on the walls of caves), the Neanderthals left us virtually nothing in this respect. There are isolated examples of objects bearing simple designs, including two engraved bone fragments from caves in Bulgaria and France. Another French cave yielded a drilled fox tooth that might have been an ornament, and the possible fragment of a flute has been reported recently from Slovenia.

Anthropologists have searched for regional differences among the stone tools produced by Neanderthals that might reflect the sort of cultural variations often evident in even the simplest of modern human artefacts. They have found remarkably little variation among tool types from different parts of Europe and the Near East. Instead, some have suggested that differences in the percentages of these generic tool types might reflect different Neanderthal cultural traditions, but recent studies of Neanderthal tools indicate that much of this variation is likely due to the degree to which an individual tool has been worn and resharpened.

There is evidence that the Neanderthals buried their dead in caves, which would seem to indicate some element of ritual and belief in their lives, but the interpretation of these burials remains controversial. Some of the skeletons seem to represent individuals who were simply buried in falling rubble and debris; whole or partial skeletons of cave-dwelling bears and other animals are not uncommon. The careful excavation of a Neanderthal skeleton discovered in France several years ago revealed no evidence of a burial pit. Some Neanderthal remains have been found associated with stone tools and other objects thought to have been grave goods; one burial found in Iraq even yielded traces of flowers (in the form of pollen concentrations) that may have been tenderly placed next to the deceased. Many anthropologists suspect that the association of these objects with the skeletons is largely fortuitous. Once again, the contrast with their modern human successors – who sometimes buried their dead with pendants, necklaces, and sculptures – is a stark one.

There have also been attempts to deduce the linguistic abilities of the Neanderthals directly from the reconstructed anatomy of their vocal tracts. These studies reveal some differences with modern humans that suggest that the Neanderthals may not have been able to produce a comparable range of speech sounds. Because no modern human language employs the full range of sounds that we are capable of making, the implications of these studies are not clear, but they do seem consistent with the general lack of evidence for the use of symbols.

The End of the Neanderthals

The last known Neanderthal to walk the earth died in southern Spain roughly 30,000 years ago, and the location of this sombre event may be significant. From that day onwards only the modern apes – safely hidden in the tropical forests of Africa and Asia – remained as living reminders of the last 10 million years of our evolution. The fate of the Neanderthals is still hotly debated among anthropologists worldwide. Were they destroyed by modern human populations, or did they mingle with the newcomers and contribute their heritage to the living peoples of western Eurasia?

Genetic studies indicate that living human populations of Europe and Asia are derived from an ancestral African population. Modern humans were present at least 100,000 years ago in Africa, and appeared shortly thereafter in the adjoining Near East. Many anthropologists believe that these people spread across Europe and Asia, replacing the Neanderthals and other archaic forms of *Homo sapiens* roughly 50,000–30,000 years ago. In fact, a widely publicized genetics study of 1987 suggested that all living humans are descended from a single African woman (the 'Eve Hypothesis'). Modern humans appear in eastern Europe over 40,000 years ago, and subsequently seem to move westward towards the Atlantic coast. Although some anthropologists insist that the modern humans of Europe are descended – at least to some extent – from the Neanderthals, there is little evidence of intermediate or hybrid forms (especially in western Europe), and the genetic contribution of the latter to the former would seem to be minimal at best.

In a physical contest between the two, it is hard to imagine the powerful Neanderthals being overwhelmed by their effete modern human counterparts. However, the invaders may have triumphed through superior organization and technology. Both the physical appearance and accompanying evidence for art and symbols indicate that the people who entered Europe roughly 40,000 years ago were fully modern in their behaviour. Our studies of the Neanderthal economy show that the two populations must have competed for the same resources.

A curious twist is that, before their arrival in Europe, modern humans revealed no signs of this new behaviour; their sites are as devoid of art and symbols as those of the Neanderthals. The change seems to have been related to the move north. The catalyst may have been the onset of the last major cold period of the Ice Age, 60,000 years ago. For all their skills in coping with northern environments, the Neanderthals seem to have had problems adjusting to the especially harsh conditions in eastern Europe. Recently dated fossils document a Neanderthal intrusion into the Near East at this time, which some believe to have been made by refugees from glacial Europe. If so, the Neanderthals may have won the first round, temporarily displacing the modern human inhabitants of the region.

During the next 20,000 years modern humans moved into eastern Europe, simultaneously manifesting their new use of symbols. Possibly the latter conferred advantages in communication and organization that were essential to settlement of glacial landscapes where resources had become scarce and widely dispersed; there is evidence (materials moved from one place to another) that the modern

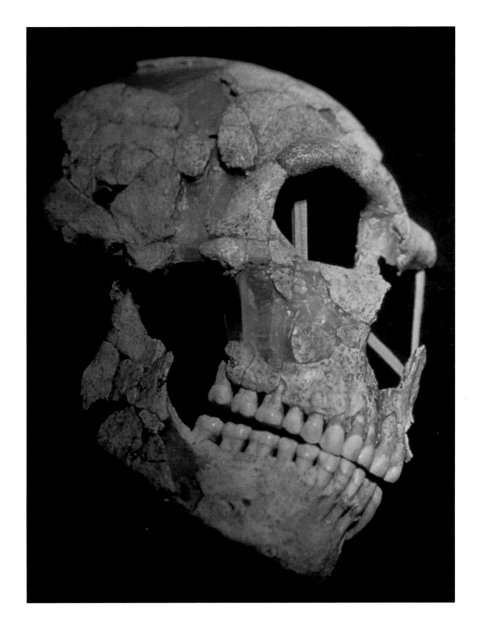

humans were foraging across much larger territories than the Neanderthals. Eventually, groups of modern humans probably intruded on lands still occupied by the latter. The encounter between the two groups, the subject of various novels and films, seems to have been protracted and complex. Some late Neanderthal sites in western Europe contain simple ornaments and tools similar to those of modern humans, suggesting that in their final period they were beginning to adopt some of the ways of the invaders. There are no traces of violence on the Neanderthal skeletons found to date, and the cause of their disappearance remains a mystery.

The youngest Neanderthal skeletons in western Europe have been found with simple ornaments and stone tools similar to those made by modern humans.

THE
ARCHAEOLOGICAL
EVIDENCE

STONE CIRCLES

AUBREY BURL

Avebury. Stones of the great south circle inside the earthwork.

Stonehenge is a wonder. It is also a contradiction. Its stones are high and heavy but they were pounded and shaped by woodworkers. No stones were available on Salisbury Plain, but determined to construct an enduring monument native carpenters dragged scores of massive sandstones from far away, up hillsides, past marshes, across moorland. They treated them like blocks of wood. Smashing, rubbing, polishing, they gave the rough slabs smooth surfaces, joints, chamfers, tenons; a ring of timber transformed into stone.

Over four thousand years ago people raised the great pillars, placed thick slabs across their tops, erected five even taller archways set like a horseshoe inside the circle. On stones at the exact east and south they carved impressions of a bronze dagger and axes, planned the ring to be in line with the midwinter sunset. The work took years, outlasting the people who began it. One marvels at their fanaticism. The accomplishment was astonishing; yet Stonehenge, for all its amazement, is only one of more than a thousand prehistoric stone circles in Britain and Ireland. They tantalize with their mysteries.

Twenty-nine kilometres north of Stonehenge is Avebury, a monster over a hundred times more spacious, its colossal stones bearing no art, standing in line with neither sun nor moon. It has no resemblance to Stonehenge and yet the rings share one grim reality. There were burials of women and children by the two entrances of Stonehenge, giving sanctity to the enclosure. A female dwarf was buried by Avebury's south entrance. Dozens of human jawbones lay in the surrounding ditch, perhaps fallen from scaffolds on which corpses had been exposed. Death was an intimate of stone circles, skeletons in central graves, cremations lying in stone-slabbed cists. In ring after ring there were human bones, perhaps sacrifices offered to the powers of nature. The burnt bones of children were discovered in the middle of the Druids' Circle in north Wales. Fragments of children's skulls were found in a pit in the middle of Loanhead of Daviot in Aberdeenshire.

Bones were obvious. Subtleties were not. It was hardly two centuries ago that a sightline to the midsummer sunrise was first detected at Stonehenge. It was not until the nineteenth century that similar alignments were noticed in other stone circles. And it is only in the last decade that other orientations have been confirmed, unexpectedly to the cardinal points of north, east, south and west, directions that remain teasingly unexplained. How they were achieved in times when there was no

Pole Star is unclear. Why they were created is debatable. What is apparent is that stone circles are far from the coarse rings of coarser stones that they have been termed in the past. It is only very slowly, with difficulty, that their secrets are being discovered. Wishful thinking has flourished, guesswork is plentiful, answers are rare.

Explanations for stone circles have differed over time. People in the Middle Ages thought the monstrous boulders had been put up by giants. By

Stonehenge. The curve of the neatly but laboriously carved lintels.

the eighteenth century giants were replaced by bloodstained Druids dragging their victims to sacrificial altars. Druids disappeared. Victorians believed the rings were observatories for astronomer-priests scientifically examining the heavens. More recently and fancifully circles became centres of extra-sensory perception transmitted from ring to ring along precisely straight lines scores of kilometres long. Even more fantastically, circles were landing-pads for the flying saucers of explorers from outer space.

Circles, Stones and Styles

There were flickers, no more than flickers, of truth in some of this. The rest were delusions based upon ignorance. Reality was simpler. Wherever there were free-lying stones and good land for farming there were stone circles. They were erected by short-lived people, most men dying in their mid-thirties, women ten years younger, but they were energetic and enterprising, clearing forests with stone axes, opening wildernesses, putting up circles in the pioneered territories. The first rings were the handiwork of groups without metal. Later, with the discovery of copper and tin, others were put up by the followers of rich and powerful chieftains with murderous bronze daggers and axes. It is the misfortune and challenge for modern investigators that those people had no writing and no understandable art, as the strange depressions and rings on the Monzie circle in Aberdeenshire show. Today we can see the stones they put up, we can recover the broken objects and the bones that they left, but these are the only clues to their needs and fears.

Adding to our problems, beliefs and customs were never identical. Even in the same region no ring was the same as another. Shapes were different, architecture and art were different, size was different. The Twelve Apostles in south-west Scotland could have accommodated 1,000 people but the shrunken Kirkhill a few miles away could hold no more than twenty. There was no comprehensive blueprint for the design of a stone circle. Despite claims for geometrical layouts and of a national measure some 0.83 metres long, adopted everywhere from the Shetlands down to Brittany, recent studies suggest that local measuring-rods, varying from community to community, are more probable.

Apart from Stonehenge, always the exception, the stones of every ring came from close by and were probably dragged on sledges by human muscle-power, levered and hauled upright into prepared holes, jammed tightly into place with stones, pebbles, clay, broken pottery – whatever was convenient. An average pillar weighed some 4 to 6 tonnes and could have been raised to the vertical by a score of labourers with the simplest of equipment: ropes, levers, antlers, and tools of wood, stone and flint. Other than the occasional shaping of the base of a stone to make its erection easier it was left in its natural state. It is noticeable, however, that it was the smoother, unweathered side that was chosen to face the interior of the circle.

Map showing main concentrations of stone circles in British Isles.

ORKNEYS

HEBRIDES

ABERDEENSHIRE

Loanhead of Daviot

Old Keig

Lundin Farm

ARRAN

LAKE DISTRICT

PEAK DISTRICT

CORK & KERRY

Rollright Stones

Drombeg

Stanton Drew

PRESELIS

Avebury

Stonehenge

BODMIN MOOR

DARTMOOR

LAND'S END

Phases

Between 3300 and 900 BC there were three important phases of stone circle building. The earliest circles were erected in the centuries before 3000 BC on moors and hillsides around the coasts of the Irish Sea and northwards along the Irish–Scottish seaways. Rings like Castlerigg in the Lake District,

Stenness in the Orkneys or Ballynoe in northern Ireland, were few but impressive. They were large, over 30 metres across, stones closely set together, had uncluttered centres, and were usually true circles. Some did have a flattened arc but this was possibly the slipshod result of a careless work-gang. Entrances to these splendid rings were marked by a

Avebury, Wiltshire. Human remains have been found here, as in other stone circles.

33

wider gap and a pair of external portals. Outside some rings was a single standing stone, like a signpost proclaiming that the land was occupied.

In the second phase, around 2600 BC, when metallurgy was introduced to the British Isles, many of

Monzie. A beautifully decorated slab outside the circle.

the most perfect circles were constructed. Some were enormous: giants like Stanton Drew, Somerset, or the Ring of Brodgar in the Orkneys were over 90 metres in diameter. The majority, however, were much smaller, between 18 and 30 metres in size. Although less grandiose they were intriguingly varied. There were circles and there were ovals whose longer axis was often set in line with a solar or lunar event. Numeracy is apparent. There was a regional tendency for a preferred number of stones whatever the length of the circumference, twelve in the Lake District, thirteen in the Hebrides, four, six and eight in central Scotland, nineteen or twenty at Land's End, five in southern Ireland.

Styles also differed. There were plain rings. There were multiple sites, such as the paired Grey Wethers on Dartmoor and the three Hurlers on Bodmin Moor. There were concentric rings, rings with stones graded in height, rings with cobbled interiors. Central pillars were set up in Cornwall and in south-west Scotland and Ireland. Imposing

avenues led to Avebury, Stanton Drew and Stonehenge. On Dartmoor rings were approached by long, meandering lines of standing stones. In the Peak District low stones stood in a rubble bank around a burial-cairn. In northern Scotland Cnoc an Liath-Bhaid, perhaps 'the stone of the grey prophet', is an outstanding oddity amongst these architectural eccentricities. On their steep hillside the stones were not put up in line along the perimeter of the ring but at right-angles across it, like the cogs of a mountain railway.

Recumbent Stone Circles

Of the many groups, one of the most informative about the customs and thinking of their makers is the recumbent stone circle tradition of Aberdeenshire. Densely concentrated in what seem to be family territories of 10.4 to 15.5 square kilometres, and erected on chosen hill-terraces that provided long views to the south, these rings – more than a hundred of them – had stones elegantly rising in height towards the south-west, where the tallest pair flanked a monstrous block lying on its side. Almost unbelievably, these gross, prostrate boulders were meticulously levelled. Even when as heavy as the 50-tonne monster at Old Keig, the vast slabs were so carefully levered, manoeuvred and set into position that even today their long, flat tops remain perfectly horizontal.

In front of them fragments of brilliantly glittering white quartz were scattered and this hints at the beliefs of those distant societies. Not only was burnt human bone deposited at the heart of the ring, but the moon was vital to the ceremonies. Small circular depressions known as cupmarks were ground out on pillars near the recumbent stone, or actually on it as at Sunhoney. The decorated standing stones were always in line with the moon, mainly at its setting. So was the recumbent, the southern moon sinking behind it, sometimes just where cupmarks had been carved. The broken quartz strewn against this 'lunar' block may have been visualized as bits of the moon itself, fallen from the heavenly body to which the dead went or from which life came.

This creates two mysteries. There are similar recumbent stone circles in south-western Ireland. Despite the hundreds of kilometres of land and sea between them the two areas share so many features

– the recumbent stone, graded heights, two high pillars, internal burials and an emphasis upon the south-west – that it must be assumed that they were related through a movement of people and ideas. The Scottish circles are thought likely to be the earlier from the pottery found in them. In Ireland rings such as Drombeg have been dated as late as 1000 BC, more than a thousand years after the first Scottish circles like Loanhead of Daviot.

The second mystery is the astronomy. Whereas the Scottish rings were aligned on the moon, the sites in Cork and Kerry were orientated on the sun – at Drombeg towards the midwinter sunset – an astronomical interest that implies that people had devised a solar calendar to record the time of seasonal gatherings. On such occasions offerings and supplications could be made to the forces of nature that threatened societies with the otherwise uncontrollable disasters of storm, drought, famine and disease. Ignorant of scientific remedies the helplessness of the people was relieved by reliance on long-tried, seemingly successful rites.

The Decline of Stone Circles

By 2000 BC the tradition of building stone circles was in decline. In this final phase new rings were built in areas not previously settled. They were usually oval or distorted; they were tiny, some no more than 3 metres across, and each region had its own character. In central Scotland ellipses of six or eight stones intermingled with sub-rectangular settings known as Four-Posters, Lundin Farm in Perthshire being a good example. In south-western Ireland in the counties of Cork and Kerry, the areas of recumbent stone circles, there were also five-stone counterparts of Scottish Four-Posters. They were squashed settings of four low boulders and an even lower recumbent, some so reduced in size that they are often obscured by reeds and grass. They were so small, the stones so diminutive that they could comfortably have been dragged into position by the few members of isolated families in the green hills of Munster.

By 900 BC faith in the usefulness of stone circles had waned. In spite of repeated rituals, a persistent deterioration in the climate year after year convinced people that circles had lost their ability to control nature. Stonehenge was abandoned. Rings were left to decay. Iron Age communities ignored

them. People in the Middle Ages avoided them as the work of the Devil. Victorian farmers removed stones for gateposts and walls. Misguided and always disappointed treasure-hunters dug gaping pits. Indifference led to neglect and today some

once-imposing rings are sadly misplaced. Sandy Road near Perth lies in an overgrown heather-bed on a housing estate. Tomnaverie recumbent stone circle in Aberdeenshire is perched above an encroaching quarry. Midmar Kirk in the same county is enclosed in a nineteenth-century churchyard. Ardblair in Perthshire has a road racing straight through it.

More positively, some circles have been rediscovered, like the one excavated by this writer on Machrie Moor, Arran, restored to the light after centuries of lying under peat. There have also been insights. Old ideas that the rings had been temples of the Druids gave way to theories that they had been observatories for astronomer-priests. Today, more believably, they are considered to have been assembly places for seasonal gatherings whose occasions were established by sightlines to the sun or moon and whose strength was enhanced by bones of the dead. The discovery of such bones, traces of fires that once flamed inside the

Midmar Kirk, Aberdeenshire. The packing-stones jammed under the recumbent stone still keep it horizontal.

rings, trampled areas where participants had entered, maybe danced, even what the rings are called are clues to the ceremonies that once took place inside them.

Ceremony, Sex and Stonehenge

The names are like whispers from a fairy-tale: the Druid's Temple, Fingal's Cauldron, Athgre-

Sabbath. These may be Christian myths but the legends of dancing and music and young women are widespread from the Nine Maidens at Land's End to Haltadans, 'the limping dance' in the Shetlands, and across to Ireland at the Piper's Stones in Co. Wicklow. As rings of stones in other parts of the world were used for ritual dancing it is possible that the names of British

Castlerigg near Keswick in the Lake District, one of the earliest stone circles.

any, 'the field of the sun', Dans Maen, 'the stone dance'. Fairies are not entirely fanciful. Elva Plain in the Lake District derives from the Old Norse *elf-haugr*, 'the hill of elves'. At the most wraithlike level of folk-memory there are the Merry Maidens, the Trippet Stones, Long Meg and Her Daughters, the Nine Ladies, all of them recording how later people believed that the stones were girls petrified for dancing on the

rings preserve recollections of the activities that once took place inside them.

It is noticeable that it is always girls that are involved, never priests. Sometimes, as at The Weddings, three rings at Stanton Drew, it was the bride, groom and bawdily roistering guests that were turned into stone, as though there was a vague remembrance not only of music and dancing but of rites of fertility between men and women to ensure the fruitfulness of the land, acts of imitative magic that the Christian church condemned as obscene. People ignored the blasphemy. As late as this century childless wives stripped naked at the Rollright Stones near Oxford to rub themselves against the life-giving male pillars. Sexual activity within the rings is likely in prehistory. Lozenge-shaped and pillar-like stones opposite or against each other at Avebury and elsewhere have been interpreted as 'male' and 'female' symbolism as though affirming the need for fecundity in people, beasts, trees and crops.

Occasionally, the stones themselves were supposed to come to life, to dance at midnight, to search for a lost partner, or to wander down to a river or stream to drink, and the association with water is important. Avenues and rows often led from a river to the circle as though water was essential to the ceremonies.

Stonehenge contains all the mysteries and some of the answers. In the beginning, over five thousand years ago, it was an unimpressive circular earthwork. It had two entrances. One, meticulously placed at the south, was a narrow causeway across the ditch and through the bank. The other, wider, at the north-east, was in line with the most northerly rising of the moon. Standing beyond the enclosure was the famous outlying pillar of the Heel Stone, midway between the moon's major and minor risings.

There was a change of cult. Man-high bluestones from the Preseli mountains of Wales below which the Gors Fawr stone circle lies were erected in two intended concentric circles inside the earthwork. The north-eastern entrance was widened for its midpoint to be in line with the midsummer sunrise. Beyond it an earth-banked avenue stretched towards the River Avon. The project was rejected. Stonehenge was changed again.

Around 2400 BC the bluestones were uprooted. They were replaced by the awesomely overbearing circle of lintelled pillars 5 metres or more high. On the outer faces of three stones at the east axe-carvings were engraved. The axis was reversed. Dawn gave way to night. The horseshoe of archways inside the ring rose towards the south-west and the midwinter sunset. Inside the cramped centre of Stonehenge, where only a few of the elite could gather, stood the tall cylinder of the Altar

Stone, likened to a phallic symbol. Outlines of weapons, a dagger and axes, were carved on a stone to the south and formalized outlines of a protectress of the dead were ground out on a pillar and a lintel to the west. A phallus carved of chalk was found near the stone. Sun, east, west, south, death and fertility all combined in the dark space at the heart of the ring, a space obscured from the unprivileged outside by the thick stones of the outer circle.

Almost three hundred brief generations have passed since the first stone circle was erected. Three thousand years have gone by since the last ring fell into disuse. Over long centuries the meanings of those sacred places were forgotten. It was a world alien to our thinking, a world in which human sacrifice may have been practised, a world dominated by the sun and moon and fear of the unexplained, a world of our forefathers whose works survive for us to admire, respect and struggle to understand.

Avebury. 'Male' pillar and 'female' lozenge stones in the Kennet avenue.

DECODING
THE STONES

STEVEN SNAPE

The Egyptian hieroglyphic script is the best-known example of a seemingly incomprehensible way of writing invented by ancient peoples, yet one which is understandable to us today. It is, however, only one of several ways of writing used by the Egyptians during their long history.

The Egyptian language changed quite considerably over 4,000 years of use, as did the scripts used to write it down. Alongside the longest lasting, the hieroglyphic script itself, which was basically used for temples, tombs and other important inscriptions, were other forms of writing, used for everyday purposes. *Hieratic* was used in parallel to hieroglyphs and was made up of abbreviated versions of the hieroglyphic signs. *Demotic* was a successor of hieratic, and used to write the developed language of the period from around 700 BC to AD 500, while *Coptic* was a script strongly influenced by Greek letters and was a form of the language used from the third century AD until the Egyptian language was superseded by Arabic during the Middle Ages. But it is the hieroglyphic script that retains the greatest fascination for us because of its nature as a form of picture-writing.

Sacred Writing

To Greek and Roman visitors, like those of today, Egypt was a land of wonders. Its temples, its pyra-

Rectangular 'serekh' containing one of the names of King Senwosret I, from the White Chapel at Karnak.

mids and its hieroglyphic picture-writing were quite unlike anything they had seen at home. Like all good tourists they were told tales about what these things meant and the stories behind them. Perhaps the most confusing and most difficult to understand were the hieroglyphics; pyramids as great tombs of despotic kings was an easy concept to grasp, but the carved images of people, animals and inanimate objects – could they really be writing? Surely there are far too many signs here to be an alphabet like that of Greek and Latin? Perhaps they are a special, non-linguistic way of conveying secret information known only to the priests within the temples: the 'Wisdom of the Egyptians'. This is a view which would find favour with a good number of people today. It is, however, wrong.

It is a misconception that began early in the study of ancient Egypt. The last hieroglyphic inscriptions were written at the end of the fourth century AD (the last dated inscription is AD 394), yet by the second half of the fifth century AD an understanding of the real nature of hieroglyphs had been lost. The author Horapollo Niliacus, seemingly a native Egyptian, wrote his *Hieroglyphica* at this time, in which he described and explained the meaning of hieroglyphic signs. It is clear from this text that at least some knowledge of hieroglyphic writing had survived, since he correctly identifies the meaning of several signs, although often with bizarre explanations of their origins. The vulture, for instance, he correctly identifies as indicating 'mother', yet says this is because 'there is no male of this species of animal'. Other explana-

tions are both bizarre and wrong: 'When they wish to show a man dead from sunstroke they draw a blind beetle, for this dies when blinded by the sun'. Unfortunately the tendency to see Egyptian hieroglyphs not as a way of writing language, but as a higher form of esoteric communication was one which greatly appealed to other Greek and Roman authors, particularly to Pythagorean philosophers, and to European scholars of the Middle Ages and Renaissance, perhaps inspired by publication of Horapollo's work in 1505. The most significant of these European scholars was the German Athanasius Kircher (1602–80), whose valuable work on the Coptic language did not inform his views on hieroglyphs, which were very much in the tradition of Horapollo in seeing the signs as full of esoteric symbolic meaning. The most famous example of Kircher's 'translations' of hieroglyphic inscriptions being that of the royal name of King Apries, which he read as 'the benefits of the divine Osiris are to be procured by means of sacred ceremonies and of the chain of the Genii, in order that the benefits of the Nile be obtained'.

Deciphering Hieroglyphs

The imperial ambitions of Napoleon Bonaparte were to prove instrumental in the decipherment of hieroglyphs. Napoleon's invasion of Egypt in 1799 brought in its wake an army of scholars determined to study this fascinating country. While

The Rosetta Stone proved to be the key to the understanding of hieroglyphs.

these savants were labouring in a deliberate search for ancient knowledge, the most significant finding was made by accident. The Rosetta Stone was found while digging the foundations for a fort near the coastal city of Rashid. The stone bears a temple decree dating to the reign of King Ptolemy V: 27 March 196 BC. Its importance is that the

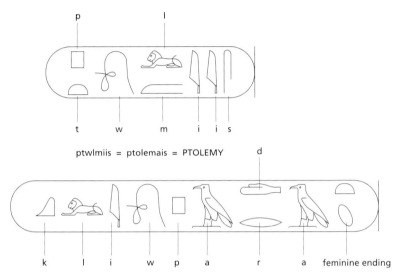

ptwlmiis = ptolemais = PTOLEMY

kliwpadra = CLEOPATRA

same text is inscribed three times on the stone: once in Egyptian hieroglyphs, with copies in Greek and demotic. The texts on the stone became the objects of determined study because the translated Greek text could act as a guide to the translation of the hieroglyphic version.

The royal names on the stone were the most obvious way into the text. It had already been correctly guessed that the groups of signs contained by the oval surround called a cartouche were in fact royal names. The English scholar Thomas Young (1773–1829) was able to identify the cartouche that corresponded to the name Ptolemy in the Greek text and work out phonetic values for the hieroglyphic signs. However, Young decided that phonetic signs were only used to write non-Egyptian names and that most hieroglyphs were of a symbolic nature. It was left to the French scholar Jean-François Champollion (1790–1832) to achieve fame as the cracker of the hieroglyphic code. Champollion began by using the now-known values of the name Ptolemy and then went on to use another bilingual Greek and Egyptian text, the Bankes obelisk, to apply these known signs to the

name Cleopatra and therefore work out the values of those signs in her name that do not appear in Ptolemy. From here it was a logical step to translate other royal names and then other words, using the Coptic language as a guide to the meaning of the decoded words.

The publication of Champollion's discoveries in 1824 marked the beginning of scholarship which was to gradually reveal the true nature of the hieroglyphic script and the language it was used to write, so that the inscriptions of the Egyptians and what they really contained could be revealed after a 'dark age' of 1,500 years.

The Use of Hieroglyphs

There is a very obvious difference between Egyptian hieroglyphs and most other scripts ancient and modern – its forms are derived from the real world and are not simply a set of distinctive, but individually meaningless squiggles like our alphabet. Staring at this page, or at the wedge-impressed surface of a cuneiform tablet, someone unfamiliar with both (say, a member of a lost tribe in the Amazon Basin) would, understandably, stare blankly at both page and tablet. However, a wall covered with Egyptian hieroglyphs would contain a whole range of familiar images; a fish, a bird, parts of the human body. The question might reasonably be asked, does this sign which looks like a bird represent something to do with a bird? The answer is sometimes yes, sometimes no. The whole nature of hieroglyphic writing is neither so simple as an obvious equation of image and real object, nor as difficult as the bizarre explanations of the Horapollo/Kircher school, but is part of a consistent and rational system of writing.

Although it may appear complex and exclusive, the purpose of hieroglyphic script was to communicate, albeit to a rather restricted audience of the Egyptian literate elite and, of course, the gods themselves. It was a form of writing developed for use in places where the beauty of the script itself was important and each sign could be lovingly crafted. This is in contrast to its cursive counterpart, hieratic, which was designed to be written quickly with a minimum number of penstrokes. Hieroglyphic was predominantly the script of the stone-carver and painter and its name (from the Greek *hieros*: 'sacred'; and *glypho*: 'sculpted') sug-

Khufu/Cheops (2251–2228 BC):
builder of the great pyramid at Giza

Amenemhat: name of four kings
of the 12th Dynasty (1991–1783 BC)

Senwosret I (1971–1926 BC):
king of the 12th Dynasty

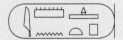

Amenhotep: name of four kings
of the 18th Dynasty (1550–1307 BC)

Tuthmosis: name of four kings
of the 18th Dynasty (1150–1307 BC)

Hatshepsut (1473–1458 BC): regent for Tuthmosis III
and ruling queen of the 18th Dynasty

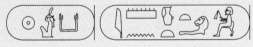

Tuthmosis III (1479–1425 BC):
warrior-king of the 18th Dynasty

Amenhotep III (1391–1353 BC):
king when Egypt's empire was at its height

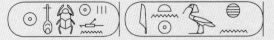

Akhenaten (1353–1335 BC):
royal religious reformer of the 'Amarna Period'

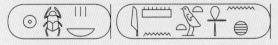

Tutankhamen (1333–1323 BC):

Ramesses II (1290–1224 BC):

Psammetichus I (664–610 BC): king of the 26th Dynasty

Nectanebo: name of two kings of the 30th Dynasty
(380–343 BC), the last native-born Egyptian Dynasty

Alexander the Great (356–323 BC)

Royal names: some of the best-known Egyptian kings.

gests that it was indeed used for texts that carried important eternal truths and used in temples (houses of the gods, built for eternity) and tombs (houses of the dead, built for eternity); the stone wall of the infinite temple carrying the infinite text. The Egyptians themselves called the hieroglyphic script *mdw nṯr* 'the god's words', and most hieroglyphic texts were records of royal activities, texts from sacred writings, lists of rituals to be performed, and wishes for the afterlife. Hieroglyphic script is used where the human world meets the divine and a permanent and distinctive expression is required to mark the event.

Hieroglyphs were therefore a very traditional form of writing and generally resistant to change, although new words do appear from time to time – inscriptions relating royal victories over foreign enemies of the New Kingdom would be hard put to dispense with the new word 'chariot'. The language of hieroglyphs was that which we call Middle Egyptian, and even when spoken Egyptian itself changed with time, hieroglyphs tended to be slow in absorbing these changes. The anachronistic nature of the language may itself have been a positive element, giving an authority to the message of the text, in the same way that the English of the King James Bible may carry extra authority for a twentieth-century reader. The script may also have had a timeless quality for the Egyptians in the same way that Latin dedicatory inscriptions were placed on the public buildings of the nineteenth century.

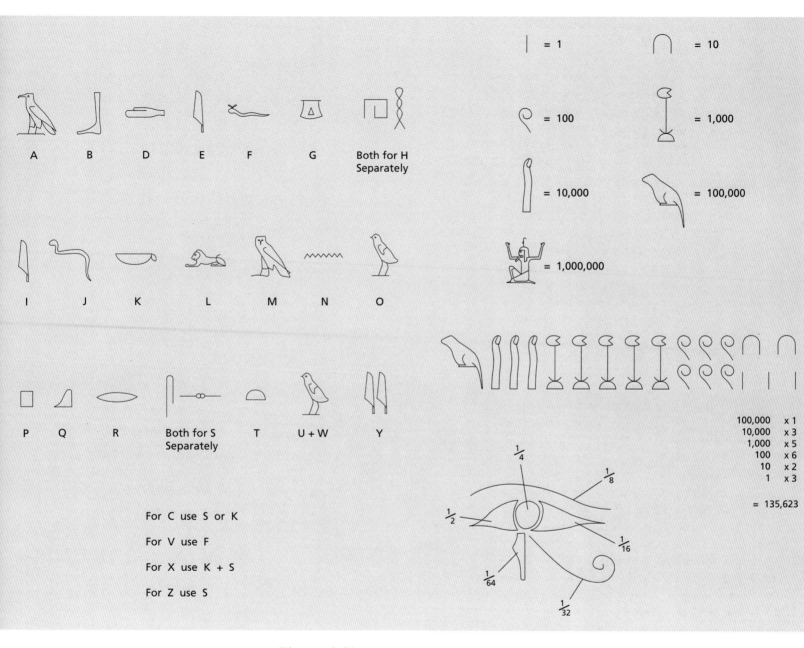

ABOVE LEFT:
Hieroglyphic 'Alphabet': some phonetic signs and their nearest equivalents.

ABOVE RIGHT:
Hieroglyphic numbers. Fractions could be formed by using parts of the eye of the god Horus.

Types of Sign

The earliest type of hieroglyphic signs are the pictorial labels attached to objects in the late Predynastic period (before 3100 BC). This is a type of 'writing' that is very easy for anyone to understand; a simple representation of, for example, a loaf of bread or a jug of beer, followed by the appropriate number of vertical strokes can represent 'five loaves of bread' or 'eight jars of beer'. By the beginning of the First Dynasty (3100 BC) the need to develop a way of representing spoken language in a written form resulted in a number of developments in the evolution of the hieroglyphic script. Two types of sign developed. The first of these was the logogram where an object was represented by a hieroglyphic sign that looked like the object itself, such as 'bull'. This is clear and straightforward, but very limiting when it comes to writing more complex sentences. For instance, on the slate palette representing King Narmer and a fallen enemy, the group of signs to the right of the king *might* be regarded as a label to the scene, reading, 'The falcon-god Horus overcomes the people of the marsh-land', or it may be a picture of that event happening – the boundary between illustration and writing is very blurred.

More complex ideas and more complex sentences would pose even greater problems. For this reason most hieroglyphic signs do not stand for the thing they look like but are employed for their phonetic value. For instance, we have already seen that Horapollo correctly identified the sign for a vulture as standing for 'mother'. The correct explanation for why this should be is the rebus principle, whereby things can be represented not by signs that look like the object, but by signs representing objects that have a similar sound. The Egyptian word for vulture was pronounced 'mwt', but the word for mother was also pronounced 'mwt'. In this way a whole range of words that were not easy to represent by single pictorial signs could be rendered by signs that were pronounced the same. This idea is already present on the Narmer palette, the name of the king himself being written with two signs, *Nar* (the nar-fish) and *Mr* (the word for chisel).

An extension of this idea was to have a range of particularly common signs that were used for their phonetic value which in English we render by one letter ([glyph] = *s*), or two letters ([glyph] = *pr*) or, less commonly, three letters ([glyph] = *nfr*). These signs are called phonograms. But phonograms and logograms are often used together in a single word, where the phonograms spell out how a word is to be pronounced, while a logogram at the end of the word acts as a determinative, making clear the meaning of a word. For example, in the verb [glyphs] *wbn*, 'to shine', the signs [glyph] = *w*, [glyph] = *b*, [glyph] = *n* and the sign [glyph] shows what the word is about. This is useful for words which sound the same but have different meanings such as the word *sr* written with the simple signs for s and r but which, according to the determinative used, can mean a type of goose ([glyph]), a ram ([glyph]), and official ([glyph]), or the verb 'to foretell' ([glyph] the appropriate determinative of a far-seeing giraffe!).

One of the benefits of the hieroglyphic system is that the text can be written from left to right or right to left in horizontal lines, or top to bottom in vertical columns. This makes it particularly suitable for inscribing individual parts of temple and tomb buildings; not just walls but columns, pillars and around doorways, where parallel inscriptions

on each side of the doorway are often direct mirror-images of each other. The direction in which the script is read is, as a rule, the direction in which the signs of the text face, but a major consideration in the arrangement of the text on the wall was its appearance, and the ability to choose one of several signs for common phonetic values facilitated a pleasing grouping of signs without unsightly gaps.

By the Ptolemaic period (332–30 BC) hieroglyphic script had become detached from the normal spoken and written language of everyday

Obelisk of Queen Hatshepsut at Karnak. In the foreground a block from a Ramesside building.

A papyrus copy of the religious text, the Book of the Dead.

Egyptians. The cursive script, demotic, was the way in which contemporary Egyptian language was written, a language that had altered considerably since the period of the Middle Kingdom, some 2,000 years before. Therefore both the hieroglyphic script and the Middle Egyptian stage of the language which it was used to write, were more and more religious and exclusive in nature. Moreover, temple inscriptions of the Ptolemaic and Roman periods developed the hieroglyphic script by the use of vastly more signs. The main purpose of this multiplication of signs seems to have been a desire to make the texts inaccessible to anyone except the initiate priests of individual temples such as Edfu, Kom Ombo and Dendera, who seem to have delighted in devising more and more cryptic ways of writing obscure myths and ritual. For instance, the normal hieroglyphic writing of the

King Ptolemy II offers a necklace to the god Osiris-Wennefer (left), on the wall of the temple at Behbeit el-Hagar in the central Delta.

FAR LEFT: *Abydos kinglist: Prince Ramesses assists his father, Seti I, in offering to the names of their royal predecessors.*

LEFT: *Standing stone stela, inscribed with a hymn to the Sun god, from the tomb of Horemheb at Saqqara.*

value t is ⌒, while at the Roman period temple of Esna the same value can be signified by…

With the end of pagan religion in Egypt, and particularly after Christianity and Christian emperors closed Egyptian temples, the reason for the existence of the hieroglyphic script came to an end and the knowledge of what hieroglyphs were and how they worked was, as we have seen, surprisingly quickly lost, only to be recovered by the determined efforts of remarkable scholars.

MUMMIES:
UNWRAPPING THE PAST

ROSALIE DAVID

The word 'mummy' was originally used to describe the preserved bodies of ancient Egyptians. It comes from the Persian word 'mumia', meaning 'pitch' or 'bitumen', a substance believed to flow from mountains in the Near East. Bitumen from the famous 'Mummy Mountain' in Persia was believed to cure diseases, and when demand exceeded supply, people turned to the preserved bodies of the ancient Egyptians, whose blackened appearance was believed to indicate that they had the same medical powers as the mumia, *and their skin tissue was used in medicine from medieval times until the nineteenth century. Thus, the word 'mummy' came to be used for these bodies, and still describes a body (skeleton and body tissues) that is naturally or artificially preserved.*

What is a Mummy?

Mummies are found in many countries, and can be preserved in many ways. Some bodies are preserved by natural circumstances: this is called 'unintentional' or 'natural' mummification, because there has been no human intervention to achieve these results – the heat or cold of the climate, the dryness of the sand surrounding the body, and the absence of air in the burial can all contribute to the mummification process, and produce varying results.

But in some countries and civilizations people also played a part in this process and intentionally increased some of the natural conditions so that the body would be better preserved. They could exclude air by providing a sealed burial place, and use additional heat sources to dry out the body tissues so that they would not decompose. The ancient Egyptians took this technique still further, and used chemical substances and other means to prevent the decomposition of the body. It is this process that is called 'true mummification' and provides the best surviving examples of mummies.

Why Did the Egyptians Mummify their Dead?

The religious beliefs and practices of the ancient Egyptians were directly influenced by the nature of the land and its climate. Herodotus, the famous Greek historian, described Egypt as the 'gift of the Nile', and it was the annual flooding of the river, rather than the scanty rainfall, which enabled some parts of the land to be cultivated. Although a

48

Valley of the Kings, Thebes, where the rulers of the New Kingdom (circa 1500–1000 BC) were buried in rock-cut tombs.

vast area of Egypt is desert, the Delta (the triangle of land through which the Nile flows to reach the Mediterranean) and the Nile Valley are fertile because of the annual river flood which, until recent times, deposited rich black mud on the river banks. Using a series of canals, the ancient Egyptians were able to irrigate an area of land where they could grow food crops and rear their animals, and they built their towns and cities in this cultivated strip. They called this area 'Kemet', meaning the 'Black Land', because of the colour of the black soil. However, beyond these fertile river banks, the desert stretched away to the horizon. The Egyptians regarded it as a place of death and terror and called it 'Deshret' (from which we get our own word 'desert'). This meant 'Red Land', and described the colour of the rocks and sand.

The Black and Red Lands symbolized both life and death, and fertility and emptiness for the Egyptians. These areas also provided the physical conditions which gave rise to mummification. The cultivable land was scarce and had to be used as a place for people to live, grow their crops and rear their animals. It was too valuable to be used for burials, and therefore, from as early as *circa* 5000 BC, it became the custom to place the dead in shallow graves on the edges of the desert where the heat of the sun and the dryness of the sand helped to preserve the body indefinitely. Before decomposition set in, the body tissues were rapidly dried out, and the sand around the corpse absorbed the bodily fluids. These 'natural mummies' are often well preserved, and the skin and hair remain on the body. The shallow graves were probably later opened up, and the preserved bodies exposed to view, by wild animals such as jackals; thus, the families and descendants of the dead became aware that the bodies retained the appearance of their relatives when they were still alive.

From around 3400 BC the burial customs of the ruling classes began to change; they were now placed in brick-lined underground chambers instead of shallow graves in the sand, and because the corpses were no longer surrounded by the hot, dry sand, they rapidly decomposed. But because people had come to believe that a person's spirit survived after death and needed to be able to return to his body within the tomb, the spirit would have to be able to recognize this body so

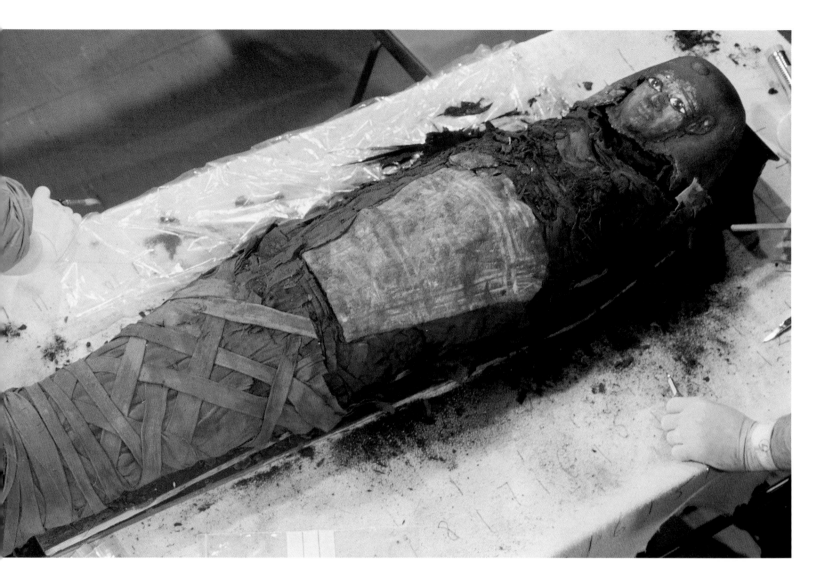

Mummy unwrapped at Manchester in 1975, showing gilded face mask and plaster chest cover (circa 100 BC, Manchester Museum).

that it could enter it and take nourishment from the food offerings which were left at the tomb. So the Egyptians had to search for alternative methods of preserving the body and retaining the individual's appearance, and for several hundred years they experimented with a range of different techniques. By about 2600 BC they had developed the process we call 'true mummification'. This was used at first for royalty, but rapidly spread to the nobility and wealthier middle classes, and continued in use for these people until Islam became the main religion of Egypt after the Arabs invaded Egypt in AD 641. Natural mummification (burial in shallow graves in the sand) continued to be used throughout this period for the poorer classes.

In the Middle Kingdom (*circa* 1900 BC), one of Egypt's most important gods – Osiris – became very powerful. Osiris was both god and king of the dead, and ruled his kingdom in the underworld, where men and women of all classes who had lived good lives were believed to continue their existence after death, cultivating the fields and crops in an eternal springtime. The annual death and rebirth of Osiris reflected the country's yearly death and revival when the flood restored the fertility of the parched land. The Egyptians believed that Osiris had been a human king who was murdered by his brother, but was ultimately restored to life as king of the dead. After his murder, Osiris's limbs were torn apart and scattered all over Egypt, but his wife, Isis, gathered them together again, and his mummification was reputed to provide the pattern for the most expensive method, carried out for those who could afford it, which was believed to ensure their own rebirth.

It was at this time too that the funerary goods placed on the body and in the tomb became so important, and they became widely available to the middle classes. The body was wrapped in many layers of linen bandages, amongst which were placed amulets (sacred charms); it was then encased in a nest of coffins. There were usually two but sometimes three of these; the innermost ones were body shaped and the outermost was rectangular. These mass-produced coffins were decorated with religious scenes and inscriptions and painted with stylized faces which did not depict the features of the individual owners. Later, in the Graeco-Roman period (*circa* first century AD), a portrait of the owner, probably painted in his lifetime and then hung in his house, was eventually cut to shape and placed over the face of the mummy.

Other traditional tomb-goods introduced in the Middle Kingdom included models (brewers, bakers, farm workers, ships and boats) which could be made full-size and brought to life by means

of magical spells, so that they could be used by the owner in the afterlife. One special group of models were the 'ushabtis', figurines of agricultural workers who would undertake duties for the owner in the land of Osiris, where the dead were expected to cultivate the crops. There were 365 ushabtis in each tomb group (one for each day of the year), plus twenty overseer figurines, to keep them in order.

As well as human mummies, the Egyptians also mummified many species of animals. They believed that a spark of the spirit of each of the many animal gods they worshipped was present in each animal. Some (cult-animals) were kept at the temples, to represent the presence of those gods on earth, and these were given elaborate burials when they died. Pilgrims to the various temples and sacred sites could also purchase specially bred and reared animals and birds kept in captivity; these would be put to death, mummified and buried in mass cemeteries, as the pilgrims' offerings to the god. If they could afford to, people also undoubtedly mummified some of their pets when they died, and encased them in wooden coffins. Cats were particularly honoured in this way, as the Egyptians regarded them as protectors of their homes.

Model boat from tomb, with mummy, mourners and sailors to enable the owner to sail to Abydos (circa 1900 BC, Manchester Museum).

How was a Mummy Made?

There are no existing Egyptian texts which tell us how mummification was carried out, and there are wall scenes in only two tombs which show some of the stages in preparing and decorating the mummy. However, two Greek writers, Herodotus (fifth century BC) and Diodorus Siculus (first century BC), have left written accounts describing the main stages of the procedure, and the mummies themselves also provide us with information about the various techniques.

According to Herodotus, three main methods were available, depending on the client's ability to pay. The most expensive was the most successful in preserving the body, and involved several stages. At death, the corpse was taken by the family to the embalmer's workshop which was situated in the cemetery area. The process apparently took seventy days to complete, although perhaps only forty days were needed for the actual mummification, and religious rituals would have occupied the remaining time.

The embalmers and their assistants probably wore masks to impersonate the gods who had attended the mummification of Osiris. A special funerary priest would have presided over the various stages, and recited the relevant religious texts. First, the body was stripped and placed on a board or platform. From at least the time of the Middle Kingdom (*circa* 1900 BC), the brain was removed through a passage chiselled through (usually) the left nostril and the ethmoid bone into the skull cavity. The brain tissue was then reduced to fragments by means of a metal hook which was introduced through this cavity. The embalmer used a kind of spatula to extract the fragments, but brain removal was usually incomplete and some tissue was left behind. Brain tissue, regarded as unimportant, was discarded, and the skull cavity was either left empty or later filled with resin or resin-soaked linen. Alternative measures were used in some mummies, where the brain fragments were either removed through the base of the skull or through a hole made in the eye socket. The eyes themselves were not removed; linen pads or artificial eyes made of obsidian or glass were inserted over the eyeballs, to make the mummy appear more realistic.

True mummification involved two basic processes – evisceration of the body and treatment of the tissues with natron, a substance which removed the bodily fluids. The body was eviscerated through an incision in the abdomen (usually placed on the left side). The viscera (internal organs) were reached through this incision, when the embalmer put his hand inside the abdomen to cut the organs free with a special knife. He removed them and then made a further cut in the diaphragm, so that he could pass his arm into the chest cavity. Here, he removed all the organs except the heart, which was left in place because the Egyptians believed that it was the thinking and feeling part of the person. Neither did the embalmer remove the kidneys, perhaps because they were difficult to reach. However, evisceration was rarely perfect or complete, and parts of the organs were frequently left behind. In some mummies there was no attempt at all at evisceration.

The extracted viscera were then dehydrated using natron. This substance, a mixture of sodium carbonate (washing soda) and bicarbonate (baking powder), combined with impurities, including salt, occurs in natural deposits in the Wadi en-Natrun, a dry valley in Egypt. The ancient Egyptians used natron for washing clothes and cleaning their teeth as well as for mummification.

Once treated and dried, the organs were wrapped in four parcels and placed under the protection of gods known as the Four Sons of Horus. The parcels were usually placed in four containers (Canopic jars) and kept in the tomb; some sets of jars have stoppers that represent the human, baboon, jackal and falcon heads of the Four Sons of Horus. In *circa* 1000 BC a new custom was introduced, and the viscera parcels, each decorated with a wax image of the appropriate deity, were replaced in the chest and abdomen cavities of the mummy.

The next stage was to dry the body. This procedure was the equivalent of modern preservative methods of embalming, involving either the injection of preserving fluids into the blood vessels, or deep freezing, or freeze-drying. Ancient techniques used either heat (sun or fire) or a dehydrating agent (natron) to remove the water content from the bodily tissues, and so prevent the growth of bacteria and the resultant decomposition of the body. In Egypt, the body was packed and covered with dry natron. This procedure, which preserved the

tissues but destroyed the grease and fat, probably lasted for forty days.

The body was then removed from the natron, and washed to remove all traces of natron and other debris. Still pliable, it was straightened out into a horizontal position so that it would fit into the coffin. During the twenty-first Dynasty (*circa* 1000 BC), the embalmers experimented with certain refinements to improve the appearance of the body. To make the shrunken body appear plumper and more lifelike, the face, neck and other areas were packed with linen, sawdust, earth, sand or butter, inserted through incisions made in the skin. False eyes were added, the body surface was painted with ochre (red for men and yellow for women), and false plaits were added to the remaining natural hair.

After the body had been dehydrated and washed, it was rubbed with oils and perfumed and coated with resin, but these were only cosmetic treatments – the essential processes which preserved the body were evisceration and dehydra-

tion. Finally, the individual limbs and the body were carefully wrapped in linen bandages and cloths, and the arms were arranged either across the chest or alongside the body. Then, in a special ceremony, a liquid or semi-liquid resin was poured over the mummy, the coffin, and the viscera in their own containers. The mummy was returned to the family, who took it, together with the dead person's funerary goods, to be placed in the tomb.

What Can We Learn from Mummies Today?

Because large quantities of human remains (skeletons and mummies) have survived, and since many people in Egypt today are the descendants of the ancient population (because there have been no major invasions by other races), it is now possible to study the pattern of some diseases which existed in antiquity and to see how they have developed over the centuries.

Various techniques are used by scientists to obtain evidence of disease in mummies. Radiology

Papyrus showing weighing of the heart, when the deceased faces the god Osiris on the Day of Judgement (British Museum).

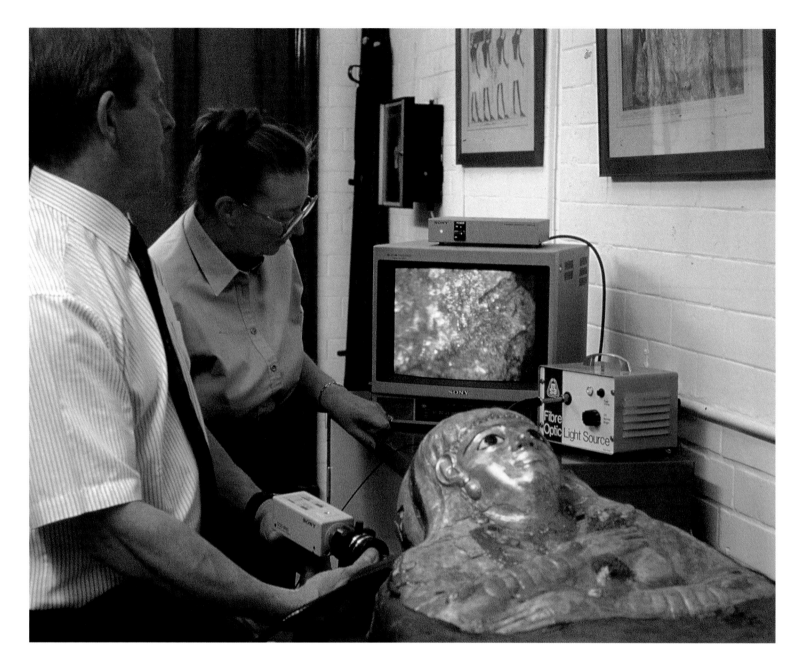

A view inside the mummy (shown on monitor), seen through an endoscope, a virtually non-destructive method of examination.

provides a totally non-destructive method: X-rays have shown the presence of disease and 'wear-and-tear' injuries in the skeleton and the remaining soft tissue. Parasitic disease caused by different types of worms is common, but cancer, syphilis, tuberculosis and rickets are rare or absent.

Using an industrial endoscope, inserted through an existing hole in the mummy, samples of tissue can be removed from deep inside the body, and sent to the laboratory where the tissue is rehydrated and then frozen, sectioned and examined under a microscope to look for evidence of disease.

An endoscope (a narrow metal tube with a light source) allows the user to look down one end and view the contents of the mummy; it also permits the researcher to gain almost non-destructive access to the mummy. This method has replaced the destructive autopsies of mummies which took place in earlier years.

Tissue obtained in this way can also be used for genetic studies. Techniques developed to identify DNA in mummified tissue now enable studies of family relationships to be undertaken. In future, it may also be possible to find evidence of bacterial,

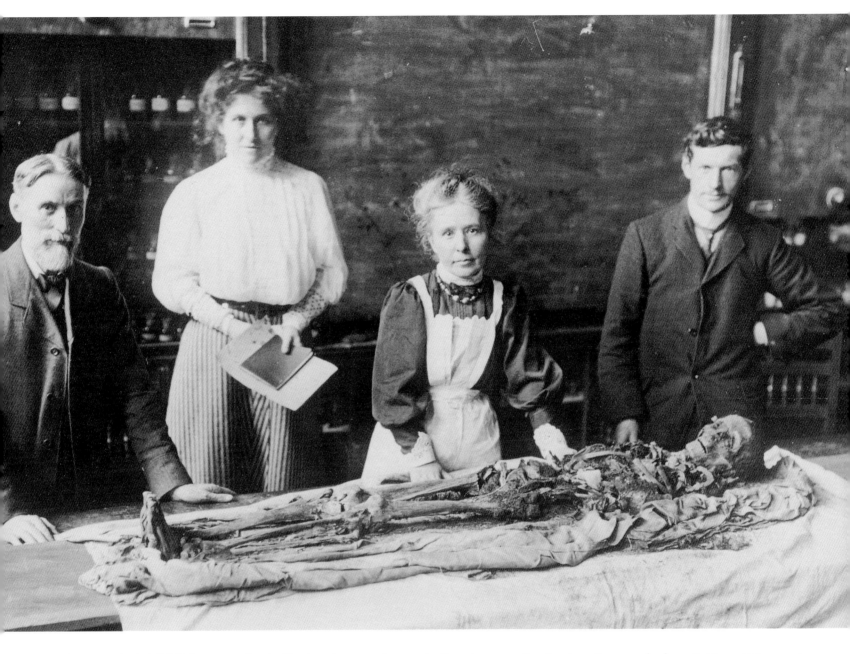

fungal and viral DNA in mummies, indicating that an individual had suffered from a particular infectious disease.

There have also been several important studies on the dental health and diet of the ancient Egyptians, and we now know that, although caries (tooth decay) was quite rare, they did suffer from severe wear of the biting surfaces of the teeth. This was the result of their diet: bread was the most popular food, and samples of bread found in tombs which have been examined show that it was heavily contaminated by windblown sand and grit

from grinding the corn. By the time they reached adolescence, most people had suffered some degree of dental wear, and the problem progressed as they became older.

By studying the mummies using these scientific techniques, we can gain a more accurate picture of their lifestyle. It is clear that they suffered from a wide range of diseases and health problems which must have affected their enjoyment of life, and this evidence must be set against the 'glamorous' image of ancient Egypt depicted in their paintings, sculpture, and literature.

Dr Margaret Murray and her team unwrap a mummy at Manchester University in 1908, pioneering research in this field.

GEOGLYPHS

PAUL G. BAHN

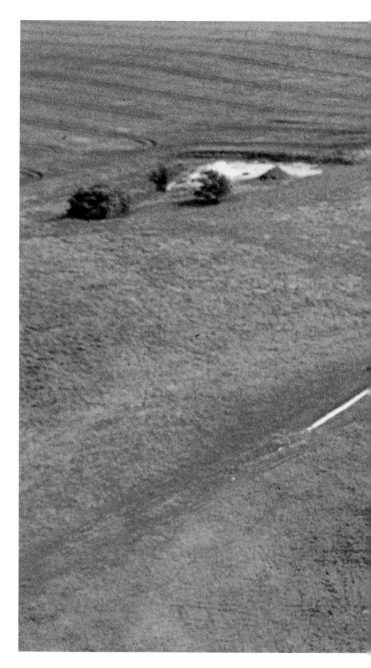

Not content with producing images – paintings, engravings, sculptures or figures pecked into rocks – of modest size, scattered around their environment, prehistoric people sometimes undertook the decoration of hillsides or even entire landscapes: a category of figure known as 'geoglyphs' or ground drawings. They include the most enormous images ever produced by our prehistoric ancestors.

Mounds and Sculptures

One kind of geoglyph involves the piling up of earth or sand into mounds to form patterns. The best known are the large prehistoric earthen mounds of the north-eastern USA, some of them built in animal shapes – for example, the Great Serpent Mound of Ohio, dating probably to the final centuries BC, which is almost 390 metres long, 6 metres wide and 1.5 metres high. It has the form of a curved serpent which seems to hold an egg in its jaws.

The Aborigines of Arnhem Land and neighbouring parts of Australia make sand or earth sculptures, during mortuary or healing rites – they include humanlike forms, images of giant fishtraps and so forth; and it is very probable that such ephemeral art forms also existed in prehistory, not only in Australia but also in other parts of the world.

Chalk Figures

Among the most famous geoglyphs in the world are the giant hill figures of Britain, images made by removing turf above chalk to make a bright white line against a green background. These figures require regular scouring to have their whiteness maintained, and to prevent being overgrown. If left untended for more than twenty years, the white lines disappear.

The two great human figures, the 'Long Man of Wilmington' in Sussex, and the very phallic 'Cerne

Abbas Giant' in Dorset are of unknown age; however, there is no doubt that the Uffington Horse in Oxfordshire, 110 metres long, is prehistoric. Long thought to be of the Iron Age, from comparisons with horse figures in Celtic art, but also ascribed by some to Anglo-Saxon times, it has now been shown, through optical dating (which shows how much time has passed since buried soil was last exposed to sunlight) of silt laid down in the lowest levels of the horse's belly, to date back to the Bronze Age, in the range 1600–1400 BC, about one

thousand years older than previously thought. Some researchers believe the animal is actually a dragon, since the flat hill in the valley below is called Dragon Hill, and there is a legend that St George killed the dragon here, and that the spot where the blood spilled is now a patch where nothing grows.

The 'Long Man of Wilmington', 70 metres tall, holds a staff in each hand, and is thought to be Europe's biggest human depiction. Thought by many to be prehistoric – possibly a warrior, or a

The Uffington White Horse in Oxfordshire.

fertility symbol deprived of genitalia by Victorian prudery – it may also be later, since there are analogies with the stance of a soldier holding two standards (on fourth-century coins) and a seventh-century belt buckle from Kent showing a warrior with a spear in each hand, while some ascribe him to medieval times. The earliest recorded evidence of his existence is a drawing from 1710. The figure was restored in 1969, having been camouflaged with green paint during the Second World War to avoid being a landmark for enemy aircraft. A trial section cut across one of the staves showed that the trench cuts through the soil but only about 5 centimetres into the chalk beneath, and is filled with chalk rubble, whereas the Uffington Horse was cut

Aerial view of the Great Serpent Mound, Ohio.

as much as a metre into the rock, and then filled with rubble – the cutting and filling have been done repeatedly since at least 600 BC. The hardness of the trench walls will have guided the scourers' tools, so that the outline will scarcely have varied through time.

The Cerne Abbas Giant is the most enigmatic of the chalk figures. He faces the sunset, and stands 55 metres high from the top of his head to the soles of his feet (almost twice as high as the Colossus of Rhodes, one of the seven wonders of the ancient world), and 65 metres high from his feet to the top of the knobbly club, 37 metres long, which

he wields with his right hand. He is naked except for what may be a belt; he has eyebrows, eyes and a mouth, with a long grassy mound for a nose; he has a nipple and three ribs at either side, placed asymmetrically, and what may be his collarbones. Finally, he displays both testicles and an erect phallus, now 7.2 metres long. However, his phallus was originally shorter. Until the late nineteenth century, the giant also had a navel, but when he was scoured in 1908 a mistake was made (probably because this area had become grassed over), and the navel was incorporated into the 4.8 metre phallus.

The giant's outline is a neatly edged trench, about 40 centimetres wide and cut about the same distance into the soil and chalk below – taking the figure's size into account, its original layout involved the digging of about 25 tonnes of chalk from almost half a kilometre of trench, a very significant amount of work.

There are still two points of deep disagreement. The first is this figure's date. Since there are no mentions of it before 1694, when parish accounts recorded a bill of three shillings 'for repairing ye giante', some historians ascribe it to that period or shortly before. Others, however, are equally adamant that it is ancient. It is hoped that optical dating, as at Uffington, will soon clarify the issue.

But if it is ancient, what or whom does it represent? Many have seen it as a Romano-British depiction of Hercules, brandishing his club, and with a (now disappeared) lion-skin on his outstretched arm. Most recently, however, it has been claimed that the left arm has a cloak dangling from it, and may even have once held a severed human head in its fist. In other words, this would be an Iron Age image of a god, a guardian of the local tribe, the Durotriges.

There were probably many more chalk figures in Britain in prehistoric times, but they have not survived. The others which can be seen are all of very recent age – for example, the Uffington Horse seems to have inspired a wave of eighteenth- and nineteenth-century white horse carvings across the Wiltshire Downs, seven of which still remain (e.g. at Alton Barnes, Hackpen Hill and Westbury). Yorkshire has the Kilburn Horse, cut in 1857 and whitened with lime; while Scotland has a late eighteenth-century horse and stag on

Desert Intaglios

Mormond Hill, Grampian. In Buckinghamshire, there are huge white crosses at White Leaf Hill and Bledlow Ridge, variously attributed to medieval monks and Cromwell's troops. The practice still continues, such as a crown cut in Kent in 1902 to celebrate the coronation of Edward VII; an aeroplane by Dover castle, cut after Blériot's cross-Channel flight in 1909; a 73-metre-long kiwi, cut by New Zealand troops on Beacon Hill, near Salisbury Plain, in the First World War; and, largest of all, a 192-metre lion cut into the hillside at Whipsnade Wildlife Park, Bedfordshire.

The most durable of all geoglyphs are the 'desert intaglios' made in rocky or desert areas by moving aside stones coated with a natural dark varnish to expose the lighter-coloured soil beneath. These exist in Australia, Chile, Arizona and California – in fact about three hundred figures of various large sizes are known in the deserts of the American Southwest alone, around the Lower Colorado River – humans, serpents, lizards, mountain lions and apparently abstract and geometric designs. One figure, nicknamed the 'Fisherman', holds a spear, its tip composed of dozens of pieces of

Geoglyphs at Tiliviche, northern Chile.

white quartz, placed close together. Radiocarbon dating of organic material growing on gravel in figures near Blythe, California, has led to claims that they were created in about AD 890.

To the local Indians, the images are living shrines made by their remote ancestors, but at least one has been used for ceremonial purposes fairly recently, with offerings of feathers, coins and buttons being deposited in small piles of stones around a stick-figure in Arizona. In northern Australia, in historic times, large designs were observed on the surface of the plains. They were made in the dry season, while the ground was still damp, by pounding the earth with stones to make it smooth. These figures, unlike the true desert intaglios, were highly impermanent, but it is probable that they were also made here in prehistoric times.

Geoglyphs are particularly numerous and

impressive in South America, notably in Chile and Peru. In northern Chile, for example, over 125 sites are known, with about 2,500 figures; the Tarapacá desert alone has forty-four geoglyphs which seem to be linked with great temporary campsites and with important caravan routes between oases and between the coastal lowlands and the highland. Some, varying from 5 to 10

bent at the elbows like Vs, and a belt. Santa Rosita has a group of stepped rhombuses. The site of Cerros Pintados has over 350 designs, including schematized humans, men on rafts, big fish and many geometric figures, notably numerous stepped rhombuses, also known as the Andean Cross. Some researchers believe that the latter was an emblem of the Tiwanaku culture (*circa* AD 600–1000),

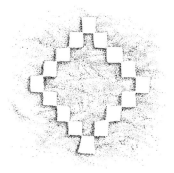

Geoglyph of a stepped rhombus, at the site of Santa Rosita, northern Chile.

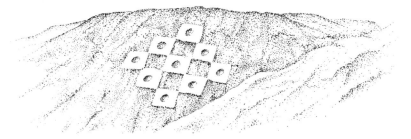

Geoglyph of a geometric figure, about 100 metres wide, at Altos de Ariquilda I, northern Chile.

Geoglyph of a stepped rhombus or 'Andean cross' from the site of Chug-Chug, northern Chile.

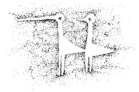

Human figure with a staff, made by piling up earth, and geoglyphs of birds at the site of Altos de Ariquilda I, northern Chile.

metres in size, mostly represent humans with sticks or supports, enclosed in circles, and animals, especially birds. Another group comprise big geometric figures (about 100 metres long), especially straight lines accompanied by or ending in volutes and meanders.

The site of El Cerro Unita has various straight lines, but also a 100-metre-anthropomorph with a radiating face, rectangular eyes and mouth, arms

marking a new area, and integrating it economically and ideologically into the Tiwanaku system and order. The design is certainly tightly linked to caravan routes, and dates back at least to the fourth century AD.

By far the best-known examples of geoglyphs, however, are the spectacular and gigantic figures on the plain at Nasca, Peru. Best visible from the air (like most geoglyphs) these images – birds, a

involvement in the Nasca layout, with the images perhaps representing constellations. After the dark, well-varnished cobbles were moved aside to make the figures, organic material accumulated on the lighter cobbles beneath and was encapsulated in new rock varnish. Radiocarbon dating of this organic matter has provided results from 190 BC to AD 660, which has been claimed to be a minimum age for the geoglyphs. This is confirmed by the distinct similarities between the animal figures and images on the pottery of the Nasca culture of AD 100–500. The Nasca 'lines' have become most associated with the work of German mathematician Maria Reiche who, from the end of the Second World War, devoted her life to them, discovering the monkey with its spiral tail, and the spider.

Many of the straight lines radiate out from single points (line centres) which are often low hilltops or ends of ridges – broken pottery found here suggests that religious offerings were made. Many of the lines seem to have served as pathways, probably for religious processions; and most of the animal figures are formed by a single line, so that one can 'enter', walk round the whole design, and 'leave' without crossing or retracing one's steps.

Experiments have shown that the straight lines were very easy to produce, with the simplest of technologies. The great animal figures – like any of the giant figures discussed in this book – were probably drawn in miniature, and then perhaps hugely expanded on to the landscape by means of a simple grid. The fact that they are best seen from above does not mean that they ever were in the past (though some have speculated, without any evidence, that the prehistoric Peruvians had the technology to make hot-air balloons). It is far more likely that they were meant to be walked, and/or to be seen by the gods. In the same way, the cruciform design of European medieval cathedrals is best appreciated from the sky, but their builders never saw them from that vantage point.

All of the varied geoglyphs in this volume have several things in common. They were produced, with great care and labour, by our ancestors, as truly monumental images of great religious or symbolic significance. And in some cases they have been deliberately maintained and renewed for centuries. Countless others must have existed, but are

Some of the hundreds of lines that criss-cross the Nasca plain.

monkey, a spider, whales, etc., up to 200 metres in size – are found amidst geometric figures such as trapezoids of 3 kilometres, as well as numerous straight lines of as much as 10 kilometres long which some believe to be ceremonial pathways, although others see a great deal of astronomical

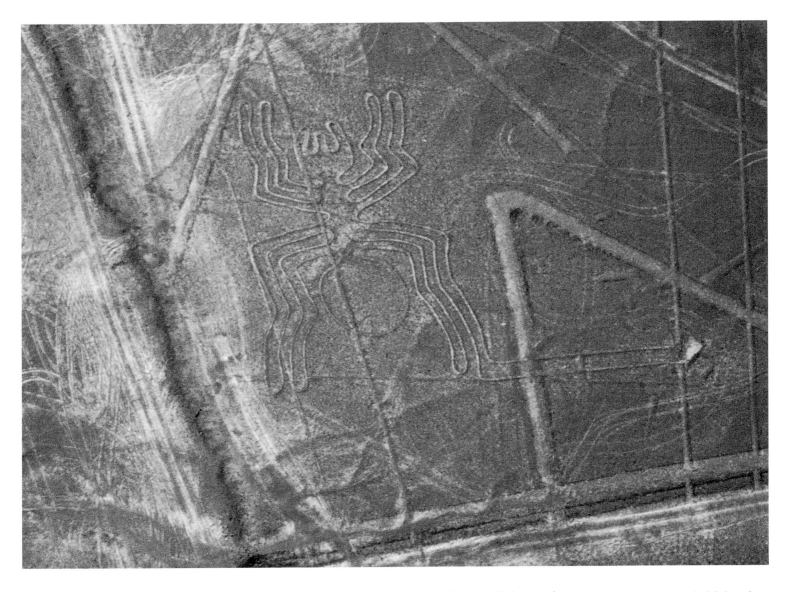

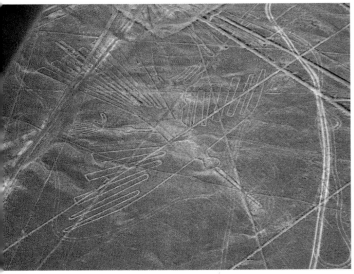

now lost for ever. Those which remain are a very fragile and precious legacy, which must be protected. Fortunately, many are in remote deserts, but even some of those (e.g. in the American Southwest) have been deliberately vandalized by people driving motorbikes or jeeps over them. Alas, just as the figures were made by simply moving the dark surface layer of stones aside, so tyres have the same effect, and the tracks and circles left by these vehicles remain as permanent scars next to the images. The only consolation is that geoglyphs are generally so enormous that it would be very difficult to destroy them completely. They are certainly among the most spectacular and impressive images ever produced by human ingenuity, imagination and sheer hard work.

ABOVE: *Aerial view of the great spider figure on the Nasca plain, 45 metres long*

LEFT: *Aerial view of one of the great humming-bird figures on the Nasca plain (its wingspan is 145 metres long).*

THE QUEST
FOR TROY

DONALD EASTON

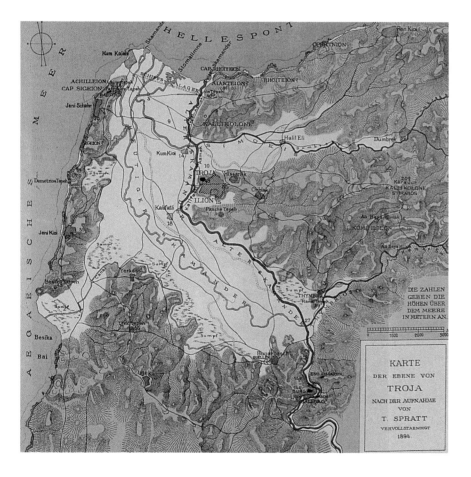

Map of the Troad: the northwest tip of Asiatic Turkey.

The stories of Troy and the Trojan War are known throughout the Western world, and have been the subject of innumerable paintings, sculptures and works of literature. The stories go back to a body of legends which circulated in classical times and are set in a heroic age, when Greece and Anatolia (modern Turkey) were divided into small kingdoms ruled by warrior-kings.

Paris, son of Priam, King of Troy (in Anatolia), had abducted the fabulously beautiful Helen, wife of Menelaus, King of Sparta (in Greece). In revenge, a coalition of Greek ('Achaean') kings set sail with 1,000 ships to raid the cities of Anatolia and besiege Troy. After ten years the siege was finally broken by a Greek ruse. Pretending to depart, they left behind a wooden horse, apparently a thank-offering to the gods; the Trojans took the horse into their city where, after nightfall, Greeks emerged from the horse's belly, opened the gates to the attackers and Troy was sacked and burned. It was a brutal victory which, however, left the Greek participants disoriented and rootless and led to the eventual collapse of the heroic age and its civilization.

Homer's Iliad

Historians in ancient Greece mainly placed the Trojan War somewhere in the period 1250–1135 BC,

and some elements of the story may go back to the second millennium BC, but crucial in bringing together some of the legends and elaborating them was the Greek poet Homer (*circa* 730 BC). Homer did not include the full story of the Trojan War in the *Iliad*. He did not, for example, include the wooden horse, although clearly this part of the legend was current at the time, as it is depicted on a vase from Mykonos dated *circa* 670 BC. Other parts of the body of legends were drawn on by other writers, most notable among whom is Virgil, the Roman poet who wrote the *Aeneid circa* 30–19 BC to celebrate the supposed descent of the Romans from the Trojans.

View from the classical site at Pınarbaşı, before Schliemann generally accepted it as the location of Homer's Troy.

At some stage the *Iliad* was committed to writing, after which it must have been copied countless times; the earliest manuscripts to survive intact come from the tenth century AD, from Constantinople. The first printed edition of Homer was produced in Florence in 1488. And so the stories of Troy and the Trojan War passed into European culture, where they became deeply embedded.

But what is the historical reality behind them? Was there a city called Troy? And did the Trojan War ever really happen?

Exploration

Homer's epic poem places Troy on the Asiatic side of the Dardanelles Straits, opposite the Gallipoli peninsula. Here, on a low ridge 5 kilometres from the sea, the inhabitants of the classical city of Ilion (730 BC onwards) believed that they lived on the site of ancient Troy. Although their city was destroyed *circa* AD 500, the name of Troy remained current in the area. Medieval travellers were shown a variety of ruins along the coast and believed that they had seen Troy.

Seventeenth-century travellers were more critical, and noticed that Homer places Troy on an inland plain, which they began to explore. The first positive suggestion for locating the site of Troy came in 1784 from Jean-Baptiste Lechevalier, who had been taking part in a French survey of the north-east Aegean. At the south end of the plain he discovered a hill above a village called Pınarbaşı. The hill had traces of ancient settlement, four burial-mounds and lay between a river and a group of springs feeding a small stream. In the river and stream Lechevalier saw Homer's rivers Simois and Scamander, in the burial-mounds he saw those of the heroes of the *Iliad*, and on the hill he placed Troy. It was a convincing identification which held the field for nearly a century.

In further survey-work in 1793, an engineer called Franz Kauffer noted a site on a ridge much closer to the sea and known to the Turks as Hisarlık. After being shown coins and inscriptions, the Cambridge mineralogist Edward Daniel Clarke correctly identified this in 1801 as classical Ilion. So the generally accepted view became that classical Ilion lay at Hisarlık while the earlier, 'Homeric' Troy lay at Pınarbaşı.

There were, however, dissenting voices. The earli-

est of these was the founder and editor of *The Scotsman*, Charles Maclaren. In an essay in the *Edinburgh Review* in 1820 he argued that the stream below Pınarbaşı was too small to be Homer's Scamander and that if, as Homer implies, Troy lay between two rivers, it could only have been at Hisarlık. This argument placed Troy on the site of classical Ilion – precisely where the ancient inhabitants and most of their contemporaries believed it to have been.

Maclaren's view, re-worked and re-published in 1863, attracted the attention of a British resident of the Troad, Frank Calvert, who happened to own a part of Hisarlık. In test excavations in 1863

and 1865 he found that Pınarbaşı was a purely classical site, but that Hisarlık had deep deposits of earlier occupation. This convinced him of the likelihood of Maclaren's identification, but he lacked the money to take the matter further. In 1868, however, he succeeded in interesting a wealthy traveller in the site, and persuaded him to start large-scale excavations. That traveller was Heinrich Schliemann (1822–90).

Excavation

The site at Hisarlık was an oval mound approximately 220 metres long and 15 metres high, resulting from the collapse and rebuilding of suc-

cessive mudbrick and stone buildings repeated over millennia.

Schliemann dug there briefly in 1870 and then in 1871–3, 1878–9, 1882 and 1890. As a newcomer to archaeology he was largely ignorant of its logic and methods, and his early work was lamentably crude. But it improved over the years, and (unusually for his day) he had the wit to engage the help of professional draughtsmen, photographers and scientists – and a brilliant architect.

His excavations removed the core of the mound to a depth of 10 metres (in places 15 metres) and in the accumulation of strata he distinguished nine broad phases. Schliemann stopped digging at 10

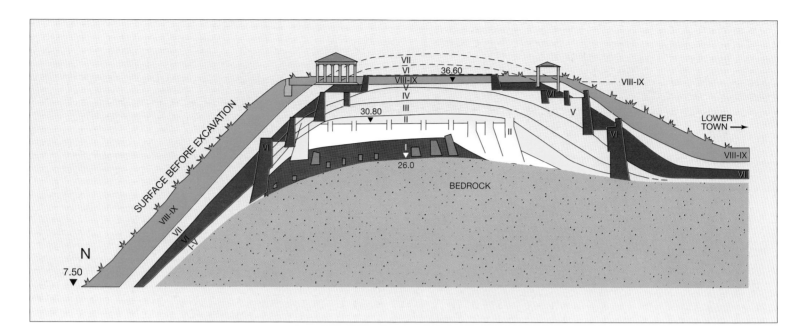

ABOVE: *Schematic section through the citadel mound of Troy (Dörpfeld, revised by Korfmann).*

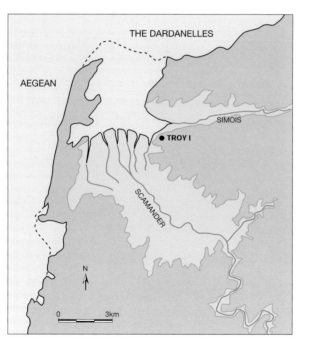

RIGHT: *Map showing the existence of a bay in the Troad in prehistoric times.*

OPPOSITE: *Fallen architectural piece being moved after having been drawn and photographed.*

later date, far more impressive than those found by Schliemann. Some of the pottery, of a type known from Mycenaean sites in Greece, enabled these buildings to be dated to *circa* 1400–1200 BC, the putative period of the Trojan War.

Dörpfeld's work gave him a clear picture of the structure of the site. Repeated building had increased the size of the mound upwards and outwards, but the top had been sliced off to build a Hellenistic temple-platform, most of which had subsequently been robbed by local peasants. Thus the remaining ruins appeared as a series of concentric rings, the innermost being the earliest.

New excavations were sponsored in 1932–8 by the University of Cincinnati, under Carl Blegen. It was a model excavation for its day, and resulted in a model publication in twelve large volumes. Blegen sampled all periods of the site's development by digging in disconnected areas untouched by Schliemann or Dörpfeld. This produced a much refined understanding of the sequence of artefacts and buildings, Blegen observing over forty phases where Schliemann had seen nine. There was, however, some difficulty in making precise correlations between his findings and those of his predecessors.

Since 1988 there have been new excavations by an international team under Professor Manfred Korfmann of Tübingen University. It is an enormous project with over one hundred archaeolo-

metres deep, because here he found impressive mudbrick buildings, all burnt, with rich collections of gold, silver and bronze metalwork. He assumed that this was Priam's Troy, the Troy of the Trojan War.

Schliemann died in 1890, and his architect Wilhelm Dörpfeld continued the excavations in 1893–4. Dörpfeld concentrated on the southern rim of the mound, mainly left intact by Schliemann. Here he found monumental stone buildings of a

Areas last dug by Schliemann

Areas last dug by Dörpfeld

Areas last dug by Blegen

Areas last dug by Korfmann (up to 1995)

Plan to show who last dug where on the citadel mound of Troy.

gists, making extensive use of modern scientific and technological methods. In the mound Korfmann is recovering a continuous sequence of strata from all periods by enlarging Schliemann's deepest and longest trench. This will provide a useful check on earlier work. He is also digging widely in the area surrounding the mound. Here a lower town of Hellenistic and Roman date has long been known to exist, but the new excavations have shown that under it there is also an entire lower town of prehistoric date. This has revolutionized our view of pre-classical Troy.

3,500 Years of Occupation

When Hisarlık/Troy was founded, before *circa* 3000 BC, the ridge on which it stood was surrounded by water. What is now the Trojan Plain was then a bay with its mouth just inside the entrance to the Dardanelles, and it was so throughout prehistory. This was Troy's greatest asset; adverse currents and winds made it extremely difficult for ships to negotiate the Dardanelles, and the bay provided a harbour where they could await a favourable wind. Troy was able to profit.

Occupation on the site is still conventionally

divided into nine broad phases. Initially (Troy I, *circa* 3000–2600? BC: all dates are still under discussion) the settlement consisted of a small group of adjoining mudbrick long-houses surrounded by a stone circuit-wall. In Troy II (*circa* 2600–2150? BC) it developed into a well-built citadel with 10-metre-high fortifications approached by a paved

2150–2000? BC). A lower town existed but its size is presently unknown.

The next phases, IV–V (*circa* 2000–1700? BC), are not so well known but appear to have been periods of quiet development. But in Troy VI (*circa* 1700–1300 BC) the site reached its apogee. There was now a magnificent fortress defended by

ramp and heavily-defended gates. This was a period of economic growth made possible partly by the introduction of the wheel. Metallurgy blossomed, and from this period come most of the twenty-one 'treasures' found by Schliemann. Within the citadel was a 35-metre-long temple or audience-hall flanked by two parallel buildings, all standing within a colonnaded courtyard with a ceremonial gateway. After a devastating fire *circa* 2350 BC, the citadel interior was covered with a maze of houses and streets – a pattern which, despite another fire, continued into Troy III (*circa*

beautifully built stone walls and towers and filled with monumental stone palaces. A lower town surrounded by ditch and palisade extended 400 metres to the South. The pottery suggests that there were close contacts with Mycenaean Greece. The artistic traditions of Troy VI survived destructions *circa* 1300 and 1200 BC (VIIa), to continue at a somewhat impoverished level (Troy VIIb, *circa* 1200–1000? BC). Signs of influence from Thrace may reflect the arrival in Anatolia of the Phrygians.

A period of abandonment followed, during

Paved stone ramp, circa 2400 BC, which led up to the principal gate of the Troy II citadel.

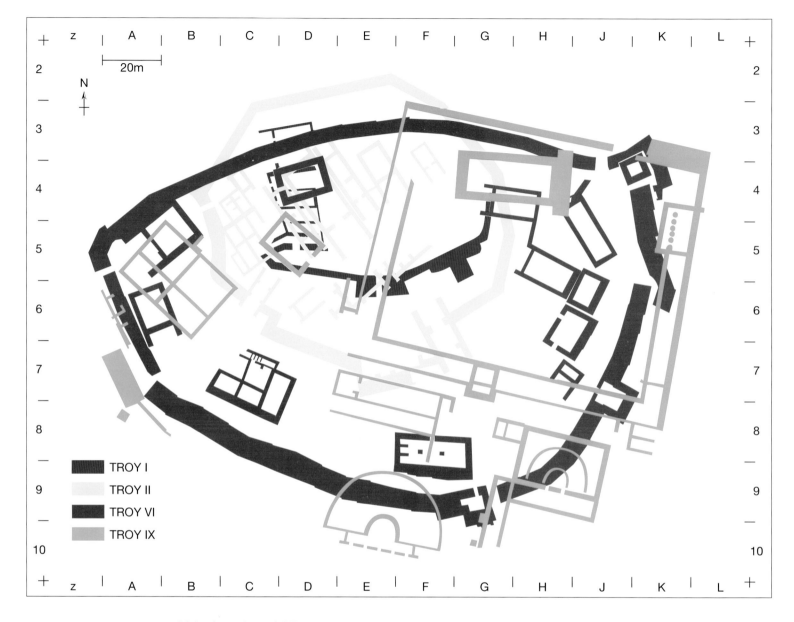

Simplified plan of the principal buildings on the citadel mound of Troy.

which the ruins of VI and VII remained visible. These perhaps became the focus of stories about the Trojan War. Then, *circa* 730 BC, around the time of Homer, the citadel was rebuilt (Troy VIII) by Greek colonizers. With other cities in the northern Troad, they had by 300 BC formed themselves into a league, erected an up-to-date theatre, temple and council chamber at Troy, and sponsored periodic games, which became an attraction to pilgrims and tourists from far and wide.

The city was attacked and burnt in 85 BC; but Rome, which regarded Troy as its mother-city, invested heavily in rebuilding (Troy IX). Most public buildings were renewed, and a water-system

was installed. The city was destroyed by earthquakes towards the end of the fifth century AD, and was only sparsely inhabited thereafter.

Missing Treasure

A mystery has surrounded the most famous finds from the excavations, Schliemann's 'treasures', which disappeared from the Berlin museums in May 1945 and vanished without trace.

These 'treasures' were twenty-one groups of metalwork: hoards of jewellery, vessels, weapons, tools and other items of gold, silver, bronze and semi-precious stones, mostly from Troy II. The largest was 'Priam's Treasure' – so-called because

The Troy II hoard of gold, silver and bronze objects found by Schliemann at Troy in 1873 – conventionally but wrongly known as 'Priam's Treasure'.

Schliemann thought that it must have been a royal treasure and that the stratum from which it came was that of the Trojan War. It has been suggested that the discovery was a hoax, and that the treasure was compiled by Schliemann from scattered finds or purchases; but the evidence is weak and the theory has little to commend it. It was almost certainly a genuine hoard, but we now know that it came from earlier than Schliemann thought: it was deliberately buried *circa* 2150 BC, nearly 1,000 years before the date usually given to the Trojan War.

Schliemann's excavation permit required him to share his finds with the Imperial Museum in Constantinople, but he smuggled most of them out of Turkey to his house in Athens. The Turks brought a case against him in the Greek courts (1874–5), which Schliemann effectively won by hiding his collection. Turkey reluctantly accepted financial compensation and apparently relinquished all claim to the objects.

Schliemann first exhibited his Trojan antiquities, including the treasures, at the South Kensington (now the Victoria and Albert) Museum in London from 1877 to 1880. He then gave them as an outright gift to the German nation, and they were exhibited in Berlin from 1882. He continued to add to them as new discoveries were made and by a massive bequest at his death in 1890.

At the outbreak of war in 1939, the Berlin museums put the most valuable items from the Troy treasures into three specially made boxes. After initial storage in museum and bank strong-rooms, in November 1941 the boxes were taken to a supposedly bomb-proof anti-aircraft tower at the Berlin Zoo. This tower was surrendered to the Red Army on 1 May 1945. The Director of the Museum of Pre- and Early History, who after the war was eventually given a senior archaeological post in East Berlin, is said to have claimed in private that he had personally handed the boxes over to a high-level Soviet commission; but few knew of this, and the truth of the claim was in any case doubted.

A chance documentary discovery in Moscow in 1987 revealed that at the end of the war the Soviet Union had pursued a policy of taking 'restitution in kind' for German looting and destruction of Soviet art works in 1941–4. A Red Army 'Trophy Brigade' of art historians had indeed taken the boxes from the anti-aircraft tower in May 1945, and had sent them by plane to Moscow. In Moscow they were held in complete secrecy by the Pushkin State Museum of Fine Arts until 1994, when a small number of western scholars (including the author) were invited to examine them.

The objects went on public display in April 1996, and remain in the Pushkin Museum. Their future is uncertain as there are impending claims for ownership from Turkey and Germany.

Has Troy Been Found?

Schliemann thought that the burnt citadel and treasures of Troy II were proof of the Trojan War's historicity. Dörpfeld thought the same of Troy VI, and Blegen of Troy VIIa. But since these three phases have little in common but their destruction, their arguments come back to a belief in the correctness of the location.

Despite all the exploration and excavation, it has never been proved that Hisarlık is the site of Homer's Troy. The only conclusive proof would be a pre-classical inscription naming the site or giving some other unmistakable indication, and such an inscription has not yet been found. But Hisarlık is in the right general location, it was an important city in pre-classical times, and its later occupants believed they were living on the site of ancient Troy. This all makes it a very good candidate.

There may be contemporary evidence for the existence of Troy from the archives of the Hittite Empire (*circa* 1600–1200 BC) at Boğazköy in central Turkey. Among the names of places in north-western Anatolia known to the Hittites is a pair which occur together: Tarwisa and Wilusa. These may be the Anatolian names underlying the Greek pair Troy and Ilios (or Ilion). Hittite texts also mention an Aegean power known to them as Ahhiya (or Ahhiyawa), perhaps the Achaea Greeks; but it is not clear exactly where Tarwisa and Wilusa lay, and the Trojan War itself is not referred to.

Although excavation has produced no texts to prove the historicity of the Trojan War, is the archaeology none the less consistent with it? For this, Troy would need to have a burnt layer of the right date. If the Trojan War took place in the thirteenth century BC, and the Achaean Greeks were what we now call Mycenaeans, then Troy VI (destroyed *circa* 1300 BC) would be a very good can-

didate. Blegen attributed its destruction to an earthquake, but on very thin evidence. Another possible candidate is Troy VIIa (destroyed *circa* 1200 BC). The destruction of this phase is most naturally attributed to 'Sea Peoples' known to have invaded Anatolia at this time; but they may well have included Mycenaeans.

The site of Hisarlık suffered many destructions throughout its history, and an earlier historical origin to the legend is also possible. Linguistically some verses in the *Iliad* predate the Mycenaean Linear B texts of the thirteenth century; and already in the fifteenth century the Hittites may have known an Anatolian song about Wilusa, possibly the same place as Troy. The Trojan War could therefore have taken place in the fifteenth century or before.

We are dealing with three different classes of evidence: from literature, history and archaeology. The three are not easy to relate. The Trojan War is known only from literature. History and archaeology neither confirm nor deny its historicity. They allow us to believe in it if we wish; but it still remains unproved.

The inner face of the Troy VI citadel wall leans over to the north. Blegen saw this as evidence for an earthquake in Troy VI.

WHO WERE
THE DRUIDS?

A. P. FITZPATRICK

The Druids. The name conjures up many images; white-robed believers at the summer solstice at Stonehenge, mistletoe, a cartoon character. All are images inspired by the ancient Druids, but who were they?

To try and solve this mystery we must look at evidence, archaeological and historical, which is 2,000 years old and dates back to the Iron Age. We shall see that the modern images of Druids are only a few hundred years old and, although they may now seem comic, they symbolize some of the first serious western attempts to understand the antiquity of humanity.

In the Renaissance the writings of the ancient Greeks and Romans became increasingly well known. Men such as Julius Caesar and Pliny described the Druids, stating that they were found in Britain and Gaul (broadly speaking modern France) and that, amongst other things, they were priests. Julius Caesar mentions human sacrifice, while Pliny describes them as worshipping in woodland groves and collecting mistletoe.

Making the Past

During the Renaissance it was increasingly realized that some features in the landscape, for example what we now recognize as prehistoric burial mounds, had been made by ancient peoples. With the 'discovery' of so-called 'primitive' peoples or 'savages' in the Americas, this gave the Renaissance thinkers intellectual and concrete materials to create an image of antiquity.

Modern scholarship distinguishes carefully between different sorts of evidence, but in the Renaissance the idea of the past was something novel, and people envisaged the past as an unchanging time either before or after the biblical Deluge. In this timeless past the different sorts of evidence could happily co-exist. The challenge for the later, Enlightenment, thinkers was to relate this past to the modern world. Mostly this was done by creating myths which related peoples, usually nations, to Noah and the Garden of Eden.

With this knowledge at his disposal John Aubrey (1626–97) wrote:

Let us imagine what kind of a countrie this was in the time of the ancient Britons . . . a shady dismal wood: and the inhabitants almost as savage as the beasts whose skins were their only raiment. The language British . . . Their religion is at large described by Caesar. Their priests were Druids. Some of their temples I pretend to have restor'd, as Avebury, Stonehenge &c. . . They were two or three degrees, I suppose, less savage than the Americans.

This was a serious attempt to build a past with the intellectual and physical materials available. Yet in Britain, at least, this was to change. After the making of this past in the Renaissance and Enlightenment, the next 200 years saw little advance in the materials available to understand it. It was, however, increasingly accepted that the ancient Britons spoke a Celtic language, allowing them to be linked with the ancient Gauls, fellow Celtic speakers.

Ironically much of this stagnation stemmed from the use made by William Stukeley (1687–1765) of Aubrey's unpublished work. Stukeley elaborated upon the idea of Druids and stone circles, and, setting his work in the context of current theological debate, saw them as purveyors of natural religion, a form of pre-Christian Christianity.

Stukeley's work set the scene for the extravagances of romanticism. Druids, now portrayed as philosophers and priests instead of 'savages', symbolized mysticism and were often viewed with nationalistic pride. An increased awareness of the heroic world of the early Irish tales in which Druids are mentioned provided the finishing touches.

Aubrey had attempted to understand the past as it might have been. Stukeley and others conjured up the origins of many of the modern images of Druids: of Druids as imagined.

The Classical Writers

Ultimately all these British attempts to illustrate the Druids drew on the writings and philosophies of the Greeks and Romans. Those works do not survive in their original form, but as copies of copies. Julius Caesar's *Battle for Gaul*, which gives the fullest account of the Druids, was written in the first century BC, but the oldest surviving version is almost a thousand years later.

These ancient sources are not insiders' views of the Druids or of Celtic societies, but those of foreigners. The act of defining the differences between peoples helps to reinforce what is unique to the people making the definitions, so the Roman writers tell us as much about how they understood their own Roman world as they do about the other peoples. As the classical world did not have a priesthood comparable to the Druids, they were often mentioned by classical writers because they were different.

Most ancient writers described the Celtic society of the time of the dramatic expansion of the Roman Empire by the conquest of western Europe from the second century BC onwards. Before conquest there was often extensive contact, diplomatic and commercial, between the classical and 'barbarian' (simply meaning non-Greek speaking) worlds; such contact could already have caused changes in the barbarian societies described by the writers.

A gold stater coin of the Aulerci Eburovices, a tribe who lived in Normandy. Just below the ear of the stylized face is a representation of a boar.

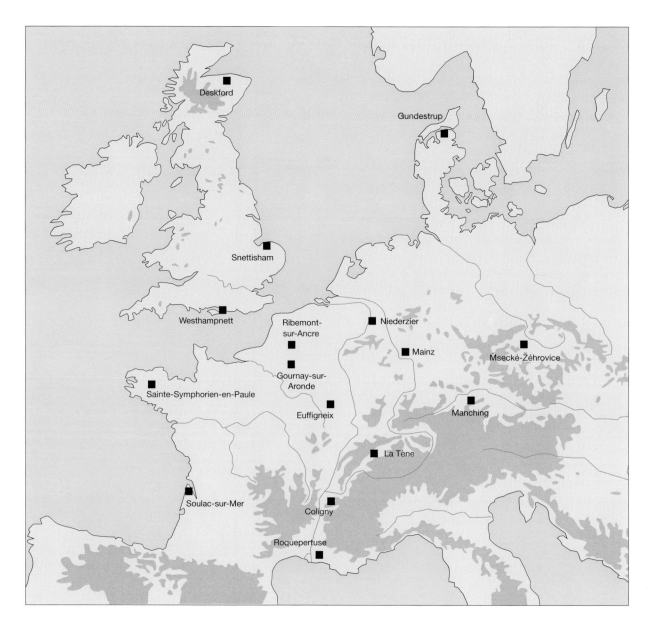

Map showing sites mentioned in the text.

The Roman authors also wrote within particular literary genres. Thus Julius Caesar's descriptions of the customs of the Britons and Gauls are in a format well-known from other enthnographic descriptions and are found half-way through *The Battle for Gaul*, indicating the importance he attached to them. Even so, we are not told the conventions used in translating Celtic ideas and words into Latin.

The earliest references to Druids are from the early second century BC, and most date to the second and first centuries BC. A smaller number come from the first century AD and mention the suppression of the Druids by Roman emperors, with a few rhetorical references in the fourth century to magicians. Most references are to Gaul, and because many classical writers copied earlier works it has often been assumed that differences between authors were due to mistakes in copying. However, it is more likely that the differences are due to changes in Celtic society and the roles of Druids over 300 years, and to local or regional differences: the first century AD writers described a situation where Gaul had been under Roman authority for a century. Allowing for this, the classical authors give a generally consistent account of a group of religious specialists, who were effectively a priesthood.

Julius Caesar described the 'only two classes of men of any account or importance' in Gaulish society as the *equites* (nobles) and the *Druidae*, or Druids. Below them in social status were the unfree *plebs* who generally did not own land. Caesar outlines three main roles for the Druids: they were in charge of religion, judges and arbitrators in disputes and teachers and keepers of knowledge.

Earlier writers also referred to *Bards* (described as poets) and *Vates* (responsible for sacrifices and divination). As described by Caesar the Druids also oversaw sacrifice and divination, so it may be that when he wrote they had assumed sole responsibility for this. Sacrifice and divination, the prediction of the future from the death-throes or entrails of the sacrificed, whether animal or human, was clearly an important role for the Druids.

Caesar translated the names of some of the Gods of the Gauls into Latin – Mercury (the god worshipped most), Apollo, Mars, Jupiter, and Minerva are named – but this tells us little of how the Gauls thought of them. He did, however, describe some beliefs:

The Druids attach particular importance to the belief that the soul does not perish but passes after death from one body to another . . . They hold long discussions about the heavenly bodies and their movements, about the size of the universe and the earth, about the nature of the physical world, and about the power and properties of the immortal gods. (*Battle for Gaul* vi, 14)

The Gauls claim that they are all descended from Father Dis; they say this is the tradition handed down to them by the Druids. For this reason they reckon periods of time, not in days but in nights . . . they go on the principle that night comes first and is followed by day. (*Battle for Gaul* vi, 18)

Julius Caesar also stated that the Druids were widely respected and powerful, and exempted from military service and taxation. Although they were literate, they did not write their teachings down, and he supposed that this was because they did not want their doctrines to be accessible to the ordinary people. Restricting access to their knowledge, which was vital at sacrifices and religious ceremonies, as well as to their roles as arbitrators and administrators of justice, would maintain their important position.

The descriptions of Druids sacrificing animals in groves and acting as healers appear later, after the

attempts to suppress the Druids, in the works of such first-century AD writers as Pliny and Mela. These suppressions may have been as much an attempt to curb the power of the Druids as keepers of knowledge and prophesy, and as arbitrators of justice, as acts of religious intolerance.

Gaul had been under Roman rule for a century by the time that Pliny speculated that the name Druid came from the Greek for oak-tree, *drus*, and wrote:

Druids – Gallic magicians – hold nothing more sacred than mistletoe and the oak tree. They choose oak groves for the sake of the tree, and never perform rites except in the presence of a

A contemporary marble portrait bust of Julius Caesar (100–44 BC). His Commentaries *on his own conquest of Gaul provide the longest account, as well as a first-hand one, of the Druids.*

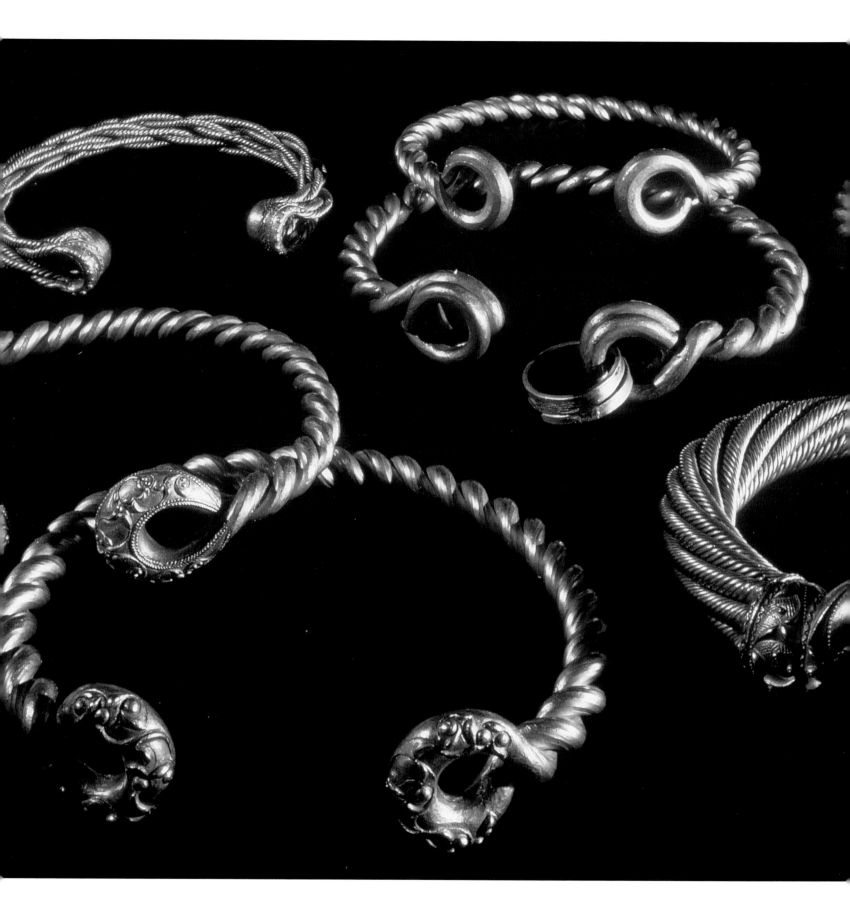

branch of it. Mistletoe is gathered preferably on the sixth day of the moon. Having feasted beneath the trees they bring forward two white bulls. A sacerdos in a white robe cuts the mistletoe with a golden sickle, and it is caught in a white cloak. The bulls are then killed. Mistletoe is known as all 'healing'. It is believed to impart fecundity to barren animals, and is used as an antidote to all poisons. (*Natural History*, xvi, 249)

Archaeological Evidence

The romantic association of Druids and stone circles and Pliny's account of the sacred grove has suggested to many that Celtic religion was practised in the open air, in natural places. Until very recently it was thought that this would have left few, if any, traces. The building of the rare temple sites like Roquepertuse in southern France, with religious statues and human skulls set in niches, could be accounted for by the long Greek and Roman contacts with the Mediterranean coast of Gaul. Indeed, some of the sites were dated to after the Roman conquest of the region late in the second century BC, the same time as some of the references to Druids.

A little archaeological evidence supports the accounts of the classical writers. The third century AD Coligny calendar, probably from a temple, was written in Gaulish which was by then an ancient language, and not Latin. It shows that time was counted in months which were either lucky or unlucky. Each month was divided in two by the word ATENOVX, when the waxing moon wanes. A few objects might be associated with Druids. Some rare short swords, so small that they are really symbolic swords, were inlaid with golden symbols which seem to represent the phases of moon. The swords may have been used in sacrifice and divination. Pairs of 'spoons' may also have been used in such rituals, but apart from this scant evidence can anything more be said?

Archaeological evidence allows us to assess the Druids or religious specialists, and Iron Age religion more generally, in different ways. Unlike the historical texts, the evidence continues to increase.

As many Greek and Roman writers referred to central and western Europe as being inhabited by Celts or Gauls (sometimes using the words synonymously), it seems that the Greeks and Romans rec-

Gold torques from Needwood Forest (top left), Ipswich and Snettisham. The Great Torque from Snettisham (bottom right) is the finest of the seventy-five more or less complete torques and fragments of 100 more, nearly all of gold but with some of silver, found in the twelve or more hoards known from the site.

index of Celtic ethnicity to illustrate them. At a broad level this may be correct but it has frequently limited archaeological interpretation to description, obscuring the many differences within the Celtic world.

For example, some religious practices were followed over large areas. The offering of hoards of gold torques and coins to the gods is found from Britain to the Czech Republic, but the types of torques, coins, and the sort of place where the offering was made is nearly always different. A sword sheath decorated with 'Celtic "art"', an art imbued with religious symbolism, might be found over much of continental Europe but the details of a find from Yorkshire declare it to be British. The man with whom it was buried, and his partner, will have lived in round houses. In continental Europe, houses were rectangular but on some settlements in Britain temples or shrines are distinguished by being square. In the second and first centuries BC cremation burial was practised over much of Europe, but the exact rites differed from region to region. In other regions inhumation burial, or ways of disposing of the dead which did not require burial, were still practised.

Later Iron Age Rituals

This diversity is also seen in the evidence for Celtic religious practices in the second and first centuries BC. This is late in the period commonly called the La Tène Iron Age after the finds made at the site of La Tène in Switzerland. Most of this evidence comes from votive deposits, sacrifices made to the gods to obtain their support or to thank them for it. Only rarely is it possible to determine what sort of god, such as of fertility or warfare, to whom the offerings were made. The gods may have had many faces or atttributes.

At the site of La Tène itself a number of bridges or jetties projected into a tributary of Lake Neuchâtel. From the third to first centuries BC weapons, particularly swords and spears, often deliberately hacked and broken, were thrown into the water. Finds of human remains suggest that people were also sacrificed. Many of the finds from this site are weapons and the placing of weaponry, much of which bears the finest 'Celtic "art"' known, in rivers or bogs is well known. The boar in particular seems to have been associated with war-

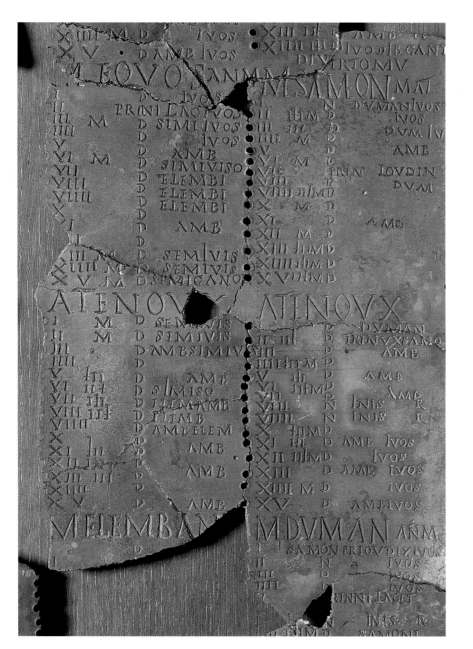

The remains of the Coligny calendar. By placing pegs in the small holes next to each day it is eventually possible to reconcile the lunar and solar years. Each month is divided into lucky and unlucky halves by the word atenovx.

ognized a broad group of peoples comparable to the German peoples or the Iberians. It is likely that many of these peoples spoke Celtic languages, but it cannot be assumed that the distribution of those modern languages called Celtic, many not recorded until the eighteenth and nineteenth centuries, is the same as their ancient distribution, or that this did not change in the intervening 2,000 years.

None the less, archaeologists were quick to link the archaeological evidence with that of the classical writers who also mentioned Celtic migrations and the linguistic evidence, using it as an

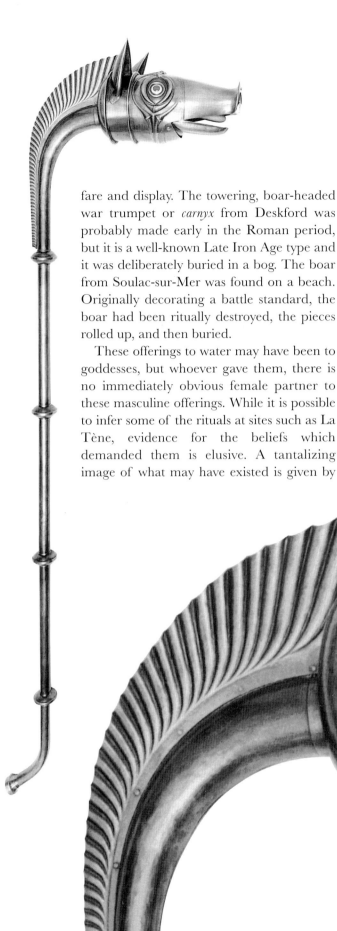

fare and display. The towering, boar-headed war trumpet or *carnyx* from Deskford was probably made early in the Roman period, but it is a well-known Late Iron Age type and it was deliberately buried in a bog. The boar from Soulac-sur-Mer was found on a beach. Originally decorating a battle standard, the boar had been ritually destroyed, the pieces rolled up, and then buried.

These offerings to water may have been to goddesses, but whoever gave them, there is no immediately obvious female partner to these masculine offerings. While it is possible to infer some of the rituals at sites such as La Tène, evidence for the beliefs which demanded them is elusive. A tantalizing image of what may have existed is given by

the myth(s) depicted on the Gundestrup cauldron. In the late second century BC this silver cauldron was dismantled and buried in a bog in Jutland, an area generally inhabited by Germanic peoples. As the cauldron was made in south-eastern Europe, there is little doubt that both the makers and users of the cauldron knew some Celtic beliefs, but the mythology it depicts, replete with elephants, may well not be Celtic.

Despite the legacy of romanticism, rivers, bogs and other 'natural' places were not the only places venerated as cult sites. In the great *oppidum* (a settlement like a town) of Manching, several shrines or temples are known, either small square or round buildings. However, a miniature tree, of wood and bronze clad in gold leaf and surely a cult idol, was buried in a pit in the settlement, not in the shrines. The small statue with a torque and lyre found at Saint-Symphorien-en-Paule, representing a bard

A modern reconstruction of the Deskford carnyx or war trumpet. This towering, boar-headed object had a range of several octaves and a wooden tongue in the mouth which could be played percussively.

Reconstruction of the boar-shaped battle standard found broken and rolled up in pieces, presumably as a votive offering, on the beach at Soulac-sur-Mer.

or, more likely, a god was also found in a settlement. It is a rare example of Late Iron Age sculpture but it also suggests that in daily life there was not a clear distinction between the sacred and the profane, and it may be here, in the home, that the seemingly absent female counterpart to the masculine offerings in 'natural' places might be found.

Although a number of statues of gods have been found in Gaul, such as the one from Euffigneix, most are likely to date to the Roman period when sacred images were required in religious ceremonies. In many cases the style of representation,

even the very idea of a physical image or idol was new. As such they are a Roman rather than Celtic way of seeing and talking about religion.

We have seen that Iron Age temples were once assumed to be rare throughout the Celtic world, yet an increasing number of Late Iron Age examples are now known. Numerous four-sided compounds, or *Viereckschanzen*, have been found in southern Germany and the Czech Republic. Some are likely to be farms, but others have shrines or temples in one corner, and deep wells which might have served as ritual shafts. The famous stone head of a god, again wearing a torque, was buried, perhaps after being deliberately broken, just outside the *Viereckschanze* at Mšecké Žehrovice.

The most important new evidence for Late Iron Age religion has come from northern France, where Roman temples were often built on the sites of Iron Age shrines. At these shrines the definition

of a sacred space by a ditch may have been more important than a house or temple for the god. Underneath the Roman temple at Ribemont-sur-Ancre Iron Age ditches enclosed a square compound, in at least two corners of which long bones, mainly of people, intermingled with weapons, were carefully stacked around a post. Nearby were the remains of headless human torsos, which may have been displayed around the edge of the compound.

At Gournay-sur-Aronde, the first Iron Age structures were aligned on the cardinal points of the (modern) compass and later on a temple was built on this alignment. The brilliant excavation and analyses of this site have shown how animal sacrifices were placed in a pit in the centre of the enclosure before their remains were carefully laid in specified places of the boundary ditch. The human remains also appear to have been dismembered, in much the same way as the numerous finds of

weapons. The reconstruction of the Iron Age temple suggested by the excavators is very similar to the types found later on in Roman Gaul. The sorts and methods of sacrifices and the precise, symbolic, use of space at Gournay-sur-Aronde reveal the site as a microcosm. It lays bare, and is a symbol for, the ways in which the ancient Gauls tried to understand their world.

The existence of cult sites such as La Tène and temples such as Gournay-sur-Aronde with their evidence for repeated rituals involving the sacrifice of people, animals and worldly goods, suggests that these sites served communities and that religious specialists may have been in charge of them.

In this respect the archaeological evidence and the testimonies of the classical writers complement each other. As well as feeding the gods, one of most important roles of blood sacrifice is divination; determining when is a good or bad time to do things. This also requires the making and marking of time, and a traditional knowledge through which to interpret the omens.

Such then is the image which emerges of the ancient Druids. Romanticism, whether ancient, modern, or New Age, has treated the Druids in the same ways as mysterious, mystic, noble and other worldly. Always as different, as 'other'. Yet they were also trying to understand their own world, their gods and their own futures. That world was very different, and it was not romantic.

The stone head of a god wearing a torque from Mšecké Žehrovice, another rare example of Celtic sculpture.

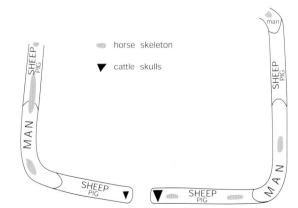

The placement of human and animal remains in the enclosing ditch at Gournay-sur-Aronde. Deposits of weapons were also carefully placed in the ditch. Drawing after Jean-Louis Brunaux.

THE MAYAN ENIGMA

CONSTANCE CORTEZ

Between the third and tenth centuries AD the Maya civilization covered the vast area now comprising Guatemala, Belize, northern El Salvador and Honduras, and the south-eastern Mexican states of Tabasco, Yucatan and Quintana Roo. The topography of the area – from the dense tropical rain forests of the lowlands to the mountainous pine forests of the Highlands – make this a truly remarkable phenomenon.

The area is hot and humid with torrential rainfalls occurring part of the year and minimal amounts of rain the rest. Despite these harsh conditions, the Maya established huge city-states ruled over by semi-divine kings. These lords were given a mandate by the gods to maintain both earthly and cosmic order. Responsibilities towards divine ancestors, the gods, and towards one's descendants were maintained through ritualized warfare and religious observances. Nowhere is the mandate from the gods more evident than in the art of two of the greatest Maya cities, Palenque and Copán.

Palenque, Mexico

The ancient city of Palenque is located in the jungles of Chiapas, Mexico. Its strategic placement, at the juncture between the lowland and highland regions greatly facilitated trade with other Maya sites and enhanced Palenque's economic importance during the Classic Period. The ruins of great temples and palaces on either side of the narrow Otulum River attest to the economic wealth of the city during its zenith (AD 600–750). Over 1,000 years of rain have washed clean the sides of the limestone structures, leaving behind only bone-white masonry. Though hard to imagine, all the structures at Palenque were once covered with smooth plaster and brightly painted, the favoured hue being red. Here and there, traces of paint indi-

cate the original palette of the ancient artists. Hieroglyphic texts carved into interior walls and under eaves recount war campaigns and the births and accessions of great monarchs. The city's florescence can be attributed to two kings: Pacal, who ruled between AD 615 and 683, and his son, Chan Bahlum who ruled between 684 and 702.

Perhaps the most famous and certainly most prominent structure at the site is Pacal's mortuary pyramid, the Temple of the Inscriptions. This building derives its modern name from the continuous text running along the back wall of the temple at its summit. Each of the pyramid's nine tiers refers to a level of the watery Maya underworld known as Xibalba (pronounced, 'she-bal´-ba'). The entire structure can be understood as a 'world mountain', a place associated not only with death but with emergence and life. The temple on top of the pyramid was metaphorically conceived of as a cave, the entrance to the underworld. It seems appropriate, then, that the stuccoed surfaces of this monument were originally painted red, the colour of life-sustaining blood.

Although locals and travellers knew of the presence

The Temple of the Inscriptions at Palenque was constructed in the seventh century by Pacal the Great as his mortuary temple.

89

RIGHT: *On the oval tablet from the palace at Palenque, Lady Zac Kuk offers her son, Pacal the Great, a headdress of royal authority.*

OPPOSITE: *The upper surface of the limestone sarcophagus lid shows Pacal falling into the open maw of the underworld.*

of the site for centuries, most of the ancient city remained covered under a densely woven shroud of vines and foliage until the late 1940s, when the Mexican archaeologist, Alberto Ruz Lhuillier began his painstaking removal of more than 1,000 years of accumulated forest growth. During his excavation and reconsolidation of the Temple of the Inscriptions, Ruz discovered a series of holes in one of the slabs which made up the floor of the temple. Removal of this slab revealed an entrance to a rubble-filled stairway. From 1950 to 1952, Ruz and his men meticulously removed the rubble from the corbel-vaulted passageway. As they progressed the excavators found caches of ceramic, jade, shell, and pearl offerings. Midway down the stairs, they uncovered the bones of half a dozen youths who had, presumably, been sacrificed in honour of the pyramid's main inhabitant.

By the summer of 1952, the workers had excavated the entire length of the internal stairway and had come to a dead end a little below plaza level. Further passage was blocked by a tightly fitted, huge triangular stone. Eventually the obstruction was dislodged and, to their surprise, the archaeologists found themselves gazing at one of the most

spectacular burials ever discovered in the New World. The vaulted crypt measured 9 metres in length, 4 metres wide, and 7 metres high and was located almost directly below the central axis of the pyramid, some 27.5 metres below the floor of the temple. Light brought into the room revealed images of nine life-size 'attendants' stuccoed to the walls, their gazes directed towards a huge limestone sarcophagus. Were these attendants placed there to stand eternal vigil over the sarcophagus, or were they somehow associated with each of the nine levels of Xibalba?

Examination of the 4-metre-long rectangular sarcophagus revealed that its surface had been carefully carved on five of its six surfaces. The lid was rolled back to expose an uncharacteristically tall male skeleton who had been adorned with jade ornaments including a jade belt and necklace. In each of his hands, he held a large jade bead. After the removal of the jade mosaic mask covering his face, another bead was found to have been placed inside his mouth. The abundance of jade artefacts can be attributed to the precious nature of the stone; for the ancients, jade represented condensed moisture, including breath, and it is probable that the jade found inside the sarcophagus guaranteed the wearer's continuation of life after death.

Outside the sarcophagus, Ruz found two life-size stucco heads which had been torn from full-length statues located elsewhere at the site. The resemblance between these heads and the mosaic mask found in the sarcophagus was striking and led scholars to believe that all of these representations constituted actual portraits of this elite individual. Still, the mystery of his identity wasn't solved until two decades later.

The 1970s represented a watershed in Maya hieroglyphic decipherment. Epigraphers working with the glyphs from Palenque were able to decipher most of the text from the Temple of the Inscriptions. They discovered that much of the information focused on a single person whose name was represented by a miniature Maya war shield. They named this individual 'Pacal', the Maya term for 'shield'. According to the ancient records, Lord Pacal had been born on 26 March 603 to Lady Zac Kuk, a member of one of the ruling families at the site. He acceded to the throne at age twelve in 615, ruling for over sixty-eight

Chan Bahlum's Group of the Cross at Palenque consists of three small temples: the Temple of the Cross, the Temple of the Foliated Cross and the Temple of the Sun.

years before his death on 31 August 683. It is believed that the sixty-nine steps on the temple's front reflect the fact that Pacal was in his sixty-ninth year of rule when he died. According to the texts, the construction of the temple began in 675 and was finally completed in 692, nine years after Pacal's death.

While the texts found throughout the site emphasize events in the life of the great ruler, the imagery carved into the surfaces of his sarcophagus provides us with insights into his spiritual beliefs. Originally painted red, the monument proclaims Pacal's ascendancy into death and his ancestry. Along the sides of the sarcophagus, the ruler's ancestors emerge from the earth as if to physically support the imagery carved across the lid's surface. On the sarcophagus lid the central image lies within a segmented rectangular border containing celestial symbols and high-ranking nobles. The hieroglyphs making up this 'Celestial Band' are associated with the moon, the sun and the planets Venus and Mars. These symbols place the central figure within a heavenly realm. While Pacal is shown falling into the gaping skeletal maw of the underworld, it was understood that after his descent into Xibalba, the king would rise again and take his place among the stars. A mirror sign, sunk into his forehead, indicates that he is depicted at the moment of his rebirth as a divinity. Jutting out from the mirror is a smoking celt (or axe), an emblem of the serpent-footed God K, a deity who is associated with lineage and the genealogical right to rule.

Pacal's placement in a personified bowl before a stylized tree is a reference to his piety. Bowls such as these were associated with the blood sacrifices offered before trees and monolithic monuments, called stelae. The tree on the sarcophagus lid represents an *axis mundi*, the centre of the world. Like many cultures, the Maya believed that such a 'world tree' stood at the centre of their cosmos. Because its branches reached into the heavens and its roots far down into the earth, this tree provided the deified dead with access into both realms. By displaying himself as a sacrifice placed before the tree, Pacal was indicating his piety and worthiness before the gods.

Because Pacal died before the temple's completion, it was left to his son, Chan Bahlum ('Serpent Jaguar'), to complete the final phases of the

The east face of Stele C, Copán, in the centre of the ceremonial court. This is a double figure, facing both east and west.

son, Chan Bahlum. The textual evidence is supported by the representation of the child himself, who is shown to have six toes on his left foot. In other representations from Palenque, Chan Bahlum is shown to be polydectile. Beyond showing himself within the context of earlier generations, Chan Bahlum visually connects himself to his father by representing himself as God K. This is indicated by his single serpent foot. Thus, while Pacal's role as an offering before the gods was emphasized within the private space of his crypt, Chan Bahlum presented himself before the Palencano populace as an incarnation of lineage blood and a legitimate heir to his father's throne.

Across the Otulum, Chan Bahlum continued to emphasize his right as legitimate heir by constructing three small temples: the Temple of the Cross, the Temple of the Foliated Cross and the Temple of the Sun. Shrines within these monuments present Chan Bahlum and his father on either side of a central icon. In the Temple of the Cross, the figures face a stylized world tree with a bird perched atop it. With outstretched arms, Chan Bahlum presents a deity to the tree, while Pacal, dressed in burial garments, holds a miniature replica of a personified offering bowl. Heraldic representation such as this has precedence in the early imagery of Hunahpu and Xbalanque, the Hero Twins of the *Popol Vuh*, the Quiche Maya Book of Genesis. Although this myth is 2,000 years old it was only recorded into European script after the Conquest. In one episode from this primordial tale, the protagonists are able to re-establish world order by shooting the vain supernatural bird, Vucub Caquix, from his perch atop a tree. Since one of the functions of Maya rulers was to maintain order on behalf of their people, it is not at all surprising that we see Chan Bahlum and Pacal take up the positions of the Hero Twins before the tree.

Copán, Honduras

Far from Palenque, Copán is situated in a valley on the Copán River in northern Honduras. For over 400 years this ancient city and the surrounding environs were under the control of a single dynasty. The first of the rulers, Yax Kuk Mo ('Blue-Quetzal-Macaw'), established his rule during the fifth century AD. Huge pyramids, stelae and altars scattered across the site's five plazas spectacularly proclaim

Temple of the Inscription. The new king had ancestors stuccoed into four of the six piers of the temple's façade. As in the case of the sarcophagus lid, the decorated piers are framed by a celestial band indicating that the scenes were spiritually charged. Each figure faces toward the temple's central entrance and holds a small child in his or her arms. On the third pier, Pacal's mother, Lady Zac Kuk, holds a baby who is named as her grand-

the successful war campaigns and histories of subsequent Copánec rulers. For example, the Hieroglyphic Stairway, containing the longest inscription in the New World, records the accessions of each of the kings up to the reign of the fourteenth ruler. Pedestals, placed at equidistant intervals along the central axis of the stairway, support life-size sculptures of five of the kings. Each figure is shown in war-associated regalia, an indication of prowess as a great warrior. Another monument, Altar Q, portrays all sixteen rulers of the site around its parameter. On the front of the altar, Yax Kuk Mo is shown handing the sceptre of authority to his descendant Yax Pac, the last great ruler of the site. On the top of this monument, the text underlines Yax Pac's legitimacy as a ruler by referencing the reign of the earliest dynast.

The Ruler 18-Rabbit

One of the most famous of the Copanec rulers, 18-Rabbit, was the subject of many of the massive stelae located in the Great Plaza. Collectively, these monuments function as a kind of symbolic forest and are referred to in their texts as *te-tunob* ('tree-stones'). Each bears the image of 18-Rabbit in the guise of a deity. On Stela D, dated to AD 736 , 18-Rabbit wears the mask of the Sun God. An oblong 'reflection sign' sunk into his forehead implies that, in this guise, the ruler took on the resplendent nature of the sun itself. This artistic format not only emphasized the semi-divine quality of the king but also his role as a living manifestation of the *axis mundi*. As was befitting all world trees, offerings would be placed on altars positioned before these tree-stones.

18-Rabbit was also responsible for the Great Ballcourt, one of the largest playing fields ever produced by the Maya. Although the exact rules of the game have been obscured by time, it is known that the event involved many players who tried to advance a rubber ball down the I-shaped field. From the imagery associated with such courts, it is also clear that the game held religious significance. According to the *Popol Vuh*, Hunahpu and Xbalanque, were the first ballplayers. When their noisy playing disturbed the lords of the underworld, they were summoned before the deities to atone for their disrespect. As the story goes, the twins survived their punishments, eventually defeated the

evil deities and were reborn as the sun and the moon. It is possible that players who lost this game were sacrificed and believed to have gone to Xibalba. There, like the twins, they would play the game for amusement of the lords of the underworld and also deliver messages from their king.

Before important events, ritual autosacrifice was performed inside of shrines within temples. The entrance to Temple 22 took the form of the open maw of a gigantic earth monster. Crossing over the tooth-lined threshold, the king would symbolically enter into a world cave. The lintel of the interior shrine represents the body of a deer-headed Celestial Monster. Its torso is defined by tiny ancestors swimming amidst streams of S-shaped blood. The head and tail of the Celestial Monster are supported by Pauahtunob, creatures responsible for holding up the sky at its four corners. After making his blood sacrifice inside of this sacred space, the ruler was able to communicate with and honour his ancestors.

Whereas 18-Rabbit's architectural campaigns were primarily focused on the northern part of the site, the monuments of Yax Pac, the last ruler of the site, were in the southern part. Both the East and West Courts symbolically represent Xibalban ballcourts. In the West Court, the flat playing field is demarcated by three square ballcourt markers bearing visages of God K. The king and his courtiers watched the play from an elevated 'reviewing stand'. At either end of the stand, anthropomorphic monkeys hold torches with T-shaped Ik signs, symbols of life and the wind. This may refer to the wind and rain-bringing clouds which were perceived to come from the cave openings. The watery nature of the underworld is indicated by the presence of God I, a fish-associated deity, and by the carved conch shells situated before him.

Likewise, the East Court had ballcourt markers indicating a playing field. Its central figure was the brother of God I, God III, a jaguar-associated deity. The W-shaped Venus signs flanking his face refer to God III's association with the planet, Venus. His placement in the East Court is significant inasmuch as Venus, in its form as morning star, was believed to pull the sun up out of the underworld. At either end of the reviewing stand, rampant jaguars dance out of Xibalba. Their now-

LEFT: *Yax Pac's last construction, Temple 18, was probably built as the ruler's final resting place. His image is located on the four internal piers of the complex.*

hollow spots once held obsidian inlay which would reflect the rising sun as it was reborn each day – a fitting reception for so important a giver of life.

Sometime during the eighth century AD, Maya sites all over Mesoamerica began to collapse. Many theories have been suggested for the abandonment of the great cities – ecological disaster, war and famine are but a few. At the site of Copán, the impending calamity is reflected in the last monuments of Yax Pac. Temple 18, Yax Pac's mortuary temple, is one of the smallest constructions at the site and stands in stark contrast to the massive monuments produced by his great ancestors. On each of its four interior piers, Yax Pac presented himself as a great warlord, wielding shield and spear and dressed in cotton armour. With the collapse of the site immanent, his attire may have reflected internal and external strife. Without supporting texts, however, it may never be known if this is an accurate portrayal of Yax Pac's capabilities as a warrior or simply wishful thinking on the part of a ruler witnessing the decline of this great city and civilization.

FAR LEFT: *The ballgame played on the surface of the ballcourt at Copán not only invoked ancient mythology, but could have deadly consequences for the players.*

97

THE VIKING SAGA

PETER SCHLEDERMANN

On an August day in 1978 I was excavating an ancient house ruin on a small island on the central east coast of Ellesmere Island in the Canadian High Arctic. The collapsed sod house had been built more than 700 years ago by Thule culture Eskimos, ancestors of all present day Inuit in Canada and Greenland.

I was removing floor debris near a stone-lined meat pit when my trowel struck a hard object. Carefully I brushed away the dirt and lifted the find up to have a closer look. I could hardly believe my eyes – in my hand I held a lump of rusted, inter-woven iron rings – a piece of medieval chain mail! Later in the day I was about to reach the bottom of the meat pit when the trowel once again struck iron – a Viking ship rivet in a thirteenth-century house ruin in the High Arctic!

Uncovering the Vikings

The discovery of chain mail was as remarkable as the fact that we had decided to investigate the island at all. The name had intrigued us, Skraeling Island, so named by a Norwegian explorer, Otto Sverdrup, who had wintered in the area between 1898 and 1899. We surmised that Sverdrup had seen Eskimo house ruins on the island, since the word *skraeling* was often used in the old Norse sagas with reference to Indians and Eskimos.

During the following field seasons we discovered many more Norse artefacts, including ship rivets, iron wedges, a carpenter's plane, pieces of woven woollen cloth, box sides made from oak, barrel bottoms, single chain-mail rings and many pieces of iron and copper. In one house we discovered a small piece of carved driftwood showing a distinctly non-Inuit face; perhaps an Inuit carving representing one of the Norsemen who had brought the many objects found in the houses? Radiocarbon dating of some of the Norse items and refuse from the winter houses implied that the dwellings had been used somewhere between AD 1250 and 1300.

The evidence left us with many unanswered questions. Where and when had the Inuit and the Norsemen first met? Had the Norsemen actually brought their ship into the High Arctic and why? Had the ship been crushed in pack ice and abandoned? Did the Norsemen winter with the Inuit on the little island and later return to their settlements in southern Greenland?

Banishment and Discovery

During the many Viking voyages between Norway and Iceland it was inevitable that the mariners occasionally got blown off course by storms in the North Atlantic. On one such occasion the sagas tell of Gunnbjorn who survived a violent gale to find himself approaching a strange, forbidding coast filled with rocky skerries. When he finally reached Iceland his story was told far and wide, eventually reaching the ears of an ill-tempered Norseman named Eirik the Red. On several occasions the quarrelsome Eirik had used his sword to settle disputes, killing a number of his opponents. In the spring of AD 982 he was tried at the local district Thing (parliamentary assembly) and banished from Iceland for three years. Eirik and his friends had little doubt about the outcome of the trial and were well prepared. His ships were loaded with livestock and food, tools and hunting gear, family and field hands, everything he needed to survive in the land he planned to investigate, the land Gunnbjorn had seen.

For three years Eirik the Red explored the south-west coast of this new land. Impressed with what he saw as he sailed along the shores of the immense fiords bordered by cascading streams and rich pastures he named it Greenland. As he sailed deeper and deeper into the fiords, he marvelled at the luxurious summer growth of grass and the size of willow thickets and dwarfed birch trees. Occasionally they came across traces of older habitations and fragments of skin boats, but never a soul came into view – the land he took possession of was empty of people. The abandoned habitations he encountered may have been occupied by Irish hermits, perhaps some of the people the Norsemen had originally enslaved or chased out of Iceland many decades before. The camps may also have been used by Dorset people, the last of the palaeo-eskimos, who occupied much of Greenland for more than 3,000 years. At the time of Eirik the Red's exploration it is very likely that some of these Dorset people still occupied the northerly regions of Greenland.

Eirik the Red returned to Iceland, where he spoke in such glowing terms about his discoveries that many chieftains decided to join him on his return to Greenland the following year. In the

spring of AD 986 a large fleet of twenty-five vessels set sail, each vessel brimming with cattle, sheep, pigs, horses, dogs, tools and food. Most of the vessels were overloaded and only fourteen completed the voyage. Eirik had already chosen the place he and his family would settle, Brattahlid, an excellent

Stone showing a Viking ship.

Skraeling Island, where the greatest concentration of Norse artefacts were found in ancient winter-house ruins, built by Thule culture Inuit.

location on the west shore of what became known as Eiriksfiord.

Not long after the first chieftains established themselves in the southernmost Greenlandic settlement they called Austerbygd, Bjarne Herjolfsson got lost on his way to Greenland. After days of drifting in thick fog he spied a low land covered with vast stretches of forest. Eventually Bjarne and his crew found their way back to Austerbygd where they told of their discovery. Eirik the Red's son Leif

was the first to explore the land to the west. He sailed along the immense, sandy shores of Markland (Labrador) and established a settlement at the northernmost promontory of Newfoundland, a place now called L'anse aux Meadows, within the territory the Norsemen called Vinland. Later explorers to the New World included Leif's brother Thorval, who was killed in battle with Indians. Leif's sister Freydis also sailed to Vinland, a voyage fraught with internal bickering and murder. One of the more impressive Norse explorers was the wealthy merchant Thorfinn Karlsefni who, with a contingent of more than 160 people, spent several years in Vinland. There his wife Gudrid gave birth to Snorre, the first European child born in the New World.

Norse Greenland

For over 200 years the Norse settlements in Greenland expanded. The original settlement by Eirik the Red had taken place during a turbulent period of Christian conversion of the Nordic lands. Eirik's wife, Thjodhild, embraced the Christian religion and arranged, under some protest from her heathen husband, the construction of a small church at Brattahlid. Over the years the Catholic Church established several monasteries and erected at least fourteen churches. In 1126 the first Bishop of Greenland, Arnald, took up residence at the Gardar episcopal seat in Einarsfiord, not far from Brattahlid.

Austerbygd contained the largest number of people and farms. Farther north on the west coast of Greenland was the settlement of Vesterbygd, with ninety farms and four churches. The seat of power in Vesterbygd was the Sandnes estate, owned at one stage by the merchant and Vinland explorer Thorfinn Karlsefni.

The Norse Greenlanders represented the westernmost outpost of European culture. They lived as crofters, raising sheep, goats and as many cattle as the irrigated homefields could sustain. Winters were long and cold and feed was often scarce. The trade link with Europe was very important to the Greenlanders, who needed iron, wood for ship building and repairs, grain and a few luxuries like silk and wine afforded only by the wealthier families. In return they could offer only a few valuable items such as walrus hides and tusks, narwhal tusks (thought to have magical properties), homespun woollen cloth and falcons, treasured by royalty and noblemen alike.

In Pursuit of Ivory

The most important hunting ground for walrus and narwhals was far north of Vesterbygd in an area the Norsemen called Nordsetur. Most scholars consider Nordsetur to be the area known as Disko Bay. The Norse hunters travelled north from

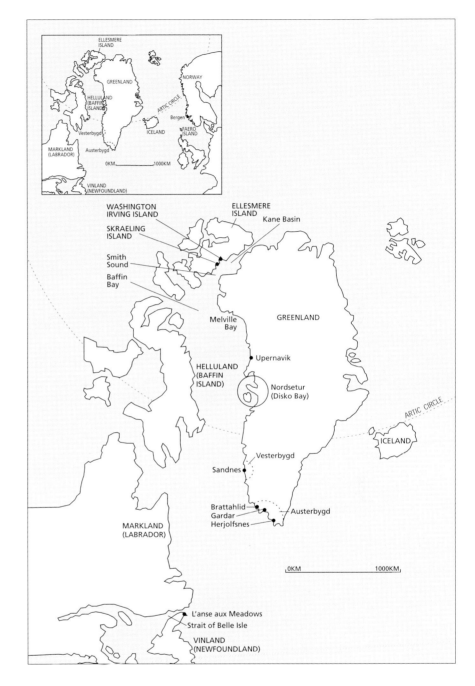

Vesterbygd and Austerbygd as soon as the frozen seas allowed passage. As the decades grew into centuries, increasing hunting pressure necessitated exploration farther northward along the rugged Greenlandic coast. The Norsemen faced other difficulties. When Eirik the Red first set foot on Greenlandic soil, the northern hemisphere was experiencing a warmer climate, with diminishing drift ice and easier navigation. A greater extent of open water in the polar seas allowed more drift-

Map showing Viking settlements in Greenland.

it difficult to maintain their meagre livestock, and indebtedness to wealthy chieftains and the Church increased.

Norse–Inuit Contact

The thirteenth century brought dangers of another kind. The Norsemen were no longer the only inhabitants of Greenland. A migration of Inuit tribes that had begun far to the west in Alaska reached the shores of Greenland. The gateway was Smith Sound, a relatively narrow, 45-kilometre-wide stretch of water or ice, depending on the season, separating Ellesmere Island and Greenland. While the Norsemen ventured farther northward in pursuit of sea mammals, the Eskimos crossed Smith Sound and began a steady push southward. It was not long before the first meetings took place between the two peoples; Inuit, superbly adapted to an Arctic way of life and Norsemen pursuing a life as farmers and hunters, a life very much rooted in another world.

The Norsemen were familiar with *skraelings*, the natives they encountered on their voyages to Vinland and Markland, where all attempts to establish permanent settlements had been successfully repulsed by the Indians. The Norsemen were easily outnumbered and carried no fighting

ABOVE: *The author uncovering a large piece of woven woollen cloth in one of the Skraeling Island houses. The cloth was later radiocarbon dated to about AD 1200.*

wood to reach the Arctic shores, providing plenty of building materials for dwellings and ships. The growth of vegetation was enhanced by the milder climate, as was the regeneration of hay-fields on the Greenlandic farms. By the turn of the thirteenth century conditions had already been deteriorating for some time, slowly at first, then more noticeably; small cottagers and landholders found

RIGHT: *Ivory needle-case from one of the Skraeling Island houses, showing, in style and decoration, that the Inuit occupants originated in Alaska.*

arms unfamiliar to the Indians, unlike the Spanish who centuries later made such a dramatic and devastating entry into Central America.

The *skraelings* from northern Greenland were different. The Norsemen must have been impressed with the Inuit sea-mammal hunting prowess. The Inuit were part of the Thule culture, characterized, among other things, by their ability to hunt bowhead whales from large skin-covered umiaqs in the open sea, and harpoon walrus and narwhals from their sleek kayaks. For the Norsemen there was good reason to offer whatever the Inuit might desire in trade for ivory and walrus skins. The Inuit may have been less interested in trade, although the Norse iron was superior to the iron flakes they obtained from meteorites in north-west Greenland.

A Norse Voyage of Discovery

The encounter with the Inuit may have encouraged the Norsemen to explore for better hunting grounds further northward. In 1814, a small, flat stone was found near three stone cairns on a small island near Upernavik, just south of Melville Bay. Inscribed on the stone was a runic message telling of three men who had constructed the nearby cairns and made the runes sometime during early spring, perhaps around AD 1300. The Norse may have travelled hundreds of kilometres north of

Although popularly held to be an aggressive people, who came by sea to raid and loot, modern scholarship has revealed other facets of the Norse character.

*Washington Irving Island
on the edge of Kane Basin,
where Captain George
Nares found two ancient
cairns in 1875.*

Upernavik. In early August 1875 the British explorer Sir George Nares had brought his two vessels, *Alert* and *Discovery*, across Smith Sound to Ellesmere Island. About 80 kilometres north of Skraeling Island he stopped in the ice near a prominent island which would provide him with a splendid view out over the ice-choked Kane Basin and the route northward. On top of Washington Irving Island he discovered, much to his surprise, two stone cairns some distance apart. Nares judged the cairns to be quite ancient because of the lichen growth on the stones. Who had constructed the cairns? After searching unsuccessfully for a message Nares and his men dismantled the cairns and built a new one. Only a few other people visited the island during the next hundred years, including a Royal Canadian Mounted Police constable, whose curiosity about the ancient cairns brought him to the top of the island in 1939.

In 1979, with more than fifty Norse artefacts in hand, we felt that the idea of Norsemen having constructed the two ancient cairns on Washington Irving Island was quite believable. Our first visit was disheartening. Not only did bad weather cut our investigation short, we discovered with great disappointment that Nares's cairn had been destroyed. In 1995 we returned to spend several days on the island. Just north of the remains of Nares's cairn we located the scattered boulders of what was undoubtedly the remains of one of the two ancient 'Norse' cairns. Our careful search of the surrounding stones and boulders did not identify the original builders – disappointing but not surprising.

One scenario may be that a small group of Norse explorers encountered Inuit hunters just south of Melville Bay. Barter led to information about fabulous sea-mammal hunting and large open-water areas to the north. The Norsemen chose to cross Melville Bay and continued northward. Seeing the tall, ice-clad mountains of Ellesmere Island only a short sailing distance away, they crossed Smith Sound and continued northward until they reached Washington Irving Island. The ice may have prevented any further progress, or massive floes of pack ice may have crushed their vessel. Two cairns were erected on top of the island followed by an attempt to return south. Inuit hunters encountered the struggling Norsemen and

– then what? Did they help them or kill them? Did they invite them to spend the winter on Skraeling Island? Were the many Norse items in the Inuit houses tokens of gratefulness or booty? We shall probably never know.

Demise of the Norse Settlements

If the Norse expedition into the High Arctic was less than successful, so was the continuation of the Norse settlements in southern Greenland. By AD 1350, the bishop's deputy, Ivar Baardsson, from Gardar in Austerbygd, could report that upon visiting the more northerly settlement, Vesterbygd, to investigate rumours of trouble with the Inuit, he had found neither heathens nor Christians in the area, although cattle and sheep had been found roaming the fields. Vesterbygd had been abandoned. If the deputy's report is at all trustworthy, and many believe it is, we are left with more questions than answers. Archaeological investigations tend to confirm that the excavated farms were abandoned about the time of Baardsson's visit. Yet, so far, we have no record of a sudden appearance of Norsemen from Vesterbygd in Iceland or anywhere else. What happened to the people?

Deteriorating climatic conditions in the thirteenth century brought increasing amounts of polar pack ice southward along the east coast of Greenland, virtually sealing off the Austerbygd coast for most of the summer. Increasing numbers of Inuit migrated southwards, competing successfully with Norse hunters. Similar competition for game took place in the autumn, when the Inuit headed inland to hunt caribou in regions used by the Norsemen.

The Inuit and the Norsemen probably engaged in barter, however there are relatively few Inuit items on the Norse farms and small amounts of Norse finds in old Inuit settlements. When the Moravians established a mission in west Greenland in the early eighteenth century, much was made of collected Inuit stories telling of fierce battles and much violence between the Norsemen and the Inuit; the Inuit burning down farms while the Norsemen attacked Inuit camps killing everyone in sight. Many of these stories are thought to be quite exaggerated. The burdens of life in the Norse colonies were also made heavier in the middle of the thirteenth century, when King Haakonsson of Norway annexed the former free state of Green-

land to his kingdom. A trade monopoly was enforced and taxation was increased. The Norse crofters were squeezed between the Church and the State, both of which expropriated farms – either in lieu of unpaid taxes or as a means of securing the owner an easier passage to Heaven. The trade monopoly resulted in fewer and fewer trade vessels touching the shores of Greenland; Europe's most westerly colony was almost completely isolated.

About the middle of the fourteenth century calamity struck Scandinavia in the form of the deadly plague that periodically ravaged most of Europe. In Norway, the most important trade centre, Bergen, was particularly hard hit. It was from here the so-called 'Greenland Knarr' departed on its infrequent trade voyages to Greenland and it may be more than a coincidence that Ivar Baardsson found no people in Vesterbygd just after the time when the plague ravaged Bergen. A late summer arrival in Vesterbygd of one trading vessel carrying plague-infested rats and fleas would have devastated the small community. No large numbers of skeletons were ever found on the excavated farms or in mass graves.

The tantalizing possibility remains that many of the Vesterbygd people headed westward to reasonably familiar territories in Labrador and the St Lawrence river area. No solid evidence supports this idea, only occasional and always controversial discoveries, such as the Kensington Stone in Minnesota, the 'Viking' tower on Rhode Island and isolated finds of coins, axes and swords. Some people are convinced that strange stone constructions and longhouse ruins on the Ungava peninsula originated with the Norse. The Vesterbygd abandonment remains a mystery.

The retreat from Vesterbygd did not end the Norse era in Greenland. In Austerbygd the Norsemen continued to work their farms and attended church services, but time was running out. The Inuit moved relentlessly southward, all the way around the southern tip of Greenland and up the east coast. The *storis* jammed the shores all summer long, preventing easy communication between farms in the inner fiord areas. Pirates had become a considerable hazard to traders in the North Atlantic. Small isolated settlements, like those in south Greenland, would have provided an easily

obtained bounty of livestock and slaves. At some time between AD 1450 and 1500 the last church bell was carefully lowered from its tower and stowed away with all other church valuables in the waiting ship; the farms were abandoned; and the Norsemen left. From their kayaks and umiaqs the Inuit may have watched the last ship sail away from the shores of what was now to be their exclusive domain, a land that had sustained the Norsemen for nearly 500 years.

Remains of the Norse Hvalso church in Austerbygd (Eastern Settlement). According to old documents a wedding took place here in AD 1408.

THE **EASTER ISLAND ENIGMA**

PAUL G. BAHN

The small speck of land now known as Easter Island is one of the most remote pieces of permanently inhabited land in the world. Roughly triangular in shape, it is entirely volcanic in origin, and covers only 171 square kilometres in the South Pacific. Yet this seemingly insignificant place has caused a huge amount of ink to flow, thanks to the amazing Stone Age culture that once filled it with enormous stone statues, many of them set up on massive stone platforms. It has often been presented to the world at large, in popular books and television documentaries, as a place full of mysteries – but research by archaeologists and others over the course of this century has finally solved most of the island's enigmas.

The First Inhabitants

The island is now generally known as Rapa Nui (Big Rapa) since nineteenth-century Tahitian sailors felt it resembled a large version of the Polynesian island of Rapa. It is so remote – 3,747 kilometres from South America and 3,622 kilometres from Pitcairn Island to the northwest – that it is extremely unlikely that it was ever colonized more

than once by people arriving in canoes, and certainly the archaeological record indicates a single unbroken development of culture from the first settlers until the arrival of Europeans. Radiocarbon dating together with evidence from linguistics, suggests that people first came here in the early centuries AD (although some researchers now believe that the arrival was some centuries later), and by the seventh century their stone structures were already well developed. Contrary to theories put forward by several people over the years, and most obsessively and persistently by Norwegian adventurer Thor Heyerdahl, the island's colonists did *not* come from South America, but rather from eastern Polynesia, almost certainly the Marquesas Islands. This is confirmed not only by archaeology and language, but also anthropology, blood groups and genetics.

Once they had reached the remote island, they were trapped there, and it constituted their whole world. Their first known contact with the rest of humanity came on Easter Sunday (5 April) 1722, when the Dutch navigator Jacob Roggeveen encountered the island, and gave it its current name. He and two of his companions were also the first to leave us written descriptions of the inhabitants. Subsequent eighteenth-century visitors included such famous explorers as Captain Cook and the Comte de La Pérouse. All of these early accounts of Easter Island marvel at the huge statues and wonder how such an apparently primitive people could move and erect such wonders on an island with no timber.

Finished statues, inside the crater of Rano Raraku, stand facing the crater lake.

Archaeological investigation of the island began in the late nineteenth century, but really came into its own in 1955 when a Norwegian expedition, led by Heyerdahl, came here, bringing in professional archaeologists. This expedition was important not only for carrying out the first stratigraphic excavations and obtaining the first radiocarbon dates and pollen samples, but also for conducting valuable experiments in carving, moving and erecting statues with the help of the islanders.

However, it was new analyses of pollen obtained in cores from the sediments at the bottom of the freshwater lakes in the island's great volcanic craters (Rano Kau, Rano Raraku, Rano Aroi) which led British palaeobotanist John Flenley in the 1980s to discover that the island was originally covered by a rainforest dominated by a species of huge palm tree very similar to *Jubaea chilensis*, the Chilean wine palm, the largest in the world.

It was to this island, totally different in appearance from that of today, that there came a group of Polynesian voyagers – probably a few dozen men, women and children in one or more big double-hulled canoes – bringing with them the domestic animals (chickens, rats, pigs and dogs) and food plants (bananas, sweet potatoes, taro, breadfruit) with which they transformed the environment of so many Polynesian islands. Breadfruit, however, could not grow in Easter Island's climate, while pigs and dogs – if they ever

Aerial view of the crater of Rano Kau.

arrived – did not survive long; their bones have never been found.

The colonists set about changing the landscape – making clearings in the forest to plant their crops. The island's native birds, unused to humans, were an easy prey to hunters, while the newly arrived rats stole their eggs and their young, so the few remaining seabirds retreated to the small islets offshore.

During this initial phase, the islanders seem to have constructed small, simple *ahu* (stone platforms) of normal Polynesian type, with small and relatively crude statues upon or in front of them.

The Construction of the Statues

In the second or 'middle' phase of Easter Island's history, seen as its Golden Age, from *circa* AD 1000 to 1500, an enormous amount of human energy

and effort was poured into the construction of more and bigger ceremonial platforms (comprising cores of rubble encased with often well-cut stone slabs) and hundreds of large statues. As the human population thrived – apparently living in peace, since there are no weapons in the archaeological record – numbers must have increased, perhaps quite rapidly: some speculate that a peak of 10,000 or even 20,000 was reached by *circa* AD 1500. This led to greater pressure on the supply of land, and the need for ever increasing quantities of food. The inevitable decline of the forest, as more land was cleared, can be seen in the record of fossilized pollen from the crater swamps. At the same time, the increasing pace and quantity of statue carving required ever greater amounts of timber for rollers and levers.

At least 800 *moai* (statues) were carved, nearly all

The long tapering fingers on this statue at Anakena make its hands look almost like wings.

of them in the soft, volcanic tuff of the Rano Raraku crater, with basalt hammerstones – thousands of which were left lying in the quarry. All of the statues were variations on a theme, a human figure with a prominent, angular nose and chin, and often elongated perforated ears containing disks. The bodies, which end at the abdomen, have arms held tightly to the sides, and hands held in front, with long fingertips meeting a stylized loincloth. They are believed to represent ancestor figures.

More than 230 *moai* were transported considerable distances from the great quarry to platforms around the edge of the island, where they were erected, with their backs to the sea, watching over the villages around each platform. It is possible that some were floated on rafts around the coast to their platform. For the rest, it has traditionally been suggested that they were dragged horizontally

to their destinations, their path lubricated with mashed palm fronds and sweet potatoes. However, recent experiments have shown that another efficient mode of transportation was upright on a sledge and rollers.

At the most prestigious platforms, the statues were given a separate *pukao* or topknot of red scoria, raised and placed on the head; and eyes of white coral, which seem to have been inserted at certain times or ceremonies to 'activate' the statues' *mana* or spiritual power. The existence of these eyes was only discovered in the 1980s; and when replicas are fitted into the sockets on re-erected statues, it transforms their appearance. The statues did not stare at the villages, but rather, their gaze was slightly upward, which may explain an old name for the island, Mata-ki-te-Rangi (eyes towards the heavens).

The Ahu Nau Nau, at Anakena, showing the statues with their stone topknots restored to them, and with reproduction eyes in place.

The statues placed on platforms range from 2 to 10 metres in height, and weigh up to 83,000 kilograms. The biggest platform was Tongariki, whose fallen remains were smashed and scattered in 1960 by a tidal wave (*tsunami*), triggered by an earthquake in Chile – indeed, its fifteen great statues, up to 30 tonnes apiece, were carried about 90 metres inland from the platform by the wave. This platform was restored in the 1990s.

The quarry at Rano Raraku still contains almost 400 statues on and around its inner and outer slopes, in every stage of manufacture. One of them, 'El Gigante', is over 20 metres long, and when completed would have weighed up to 274,000 kilograms. Many doubt that even the ingenious islanders could have moved this colossus, had it been completed, let alone have erected it.

It is the finished statues that stand on the quarry's slopes (many more probably lie buried and undiscovered here), and they have been covered by accumulated sediments up to their necks over time, and hence have given rise to the popular misconception of 'Easter Island heads', so beloved of cartoonists. They are all, in fact, full statues down to the abdomen.

A carving of a birdman, with vulva motifs, from Orongo: 46 centimetres high, 31 centimetres wide, 23 centimetres thick.

The Decline of a Civilization

The final phase of the island's prehistory saw the collapse of the earlier way of life: statues ceased to be carved, cremation gave way to burial, and 1,000 years of peaceful coexistence were shattered by the manufacture in huge quantities of *mataa*, spearheads and daggers of obsidian, a sharp, black volcanic glass. Conflict seems to have led to the toppling of the statues – some researchers have recently suggested that an earthquake might have been at least partially responsible, but there is no evidence of this at all in the island's folk-tales, and such a shattering experience in such recent times would certainly have left its mark in legend and song, as the human strife did.

The conflict was resolved by an apparent abandonment of the earlier religion and social system based on ancestor worship, in favour of one featuring a warrior elite. An annual chief or 'birdman' was chosen each year at the ceremonial village of Orongo, whose drystone corbelled houses were perched high on the cliff separating the great Rano Kau crater from the ocean. Each candidate had a young man to represent him. Every spring, these unfortunate young men had to descend the sheer cliff 300 metres high, to the shore, then swim over a kilometre on a bunch of reeds through shark-infested swells and strong currents to the largest and outermost islet, Motu Nui, where they awaited – sometimes for weeks – the arrival of a migratory seabird, the sooty tern. The aim was to find its first egg. The winner would swim back with the egg securely held in a headband, and his master would become the new sacred birdman. Orongo's rich rock art is festooned with carvings of the birdmen, sometimes holding the egg, which symbolized fertility. This was the system that was still developing when the Europeans turned up, and which ended with the arrival of missionaries in the 1860s.

Rongorongo

It seems to have been the arrival of Europeans which brought about Easter Island's last great mystery, the famous *rongorongo* writing, since we have no evidence of its existence before that time. The script comprises parallel lines of characters, many of them bird symbols, hooks, etc., engraved on

wooden tablets. Every alternate line is upside down, and the overall impression is of a tightly packed mass of uniform, skilfully inscribed hieroglyphics. Not one of the early European visitors who came to the island after its discovery by the outside world in 1722 ever mentioned the wooden tablets or the characters, although some spent days exploring ashore and entered native houses. The earliest written mention of the phenomenon is by a missionary in 1864, who said they were to be found in every house. Later visitors reported that they were kept apart in special houses and were very strictly taboo. It seems most likely that the 'script' was a very late phenomenon, directly inspired by the visit of the Spanish in 1770, when a written proclamation of annexation was offered to the chiefs and priests to be 'signed in their native characters'. This was probably their first experience of speech embodied in parallel lines, and they

ABOVE: *The rongorongo tablet known as the 'Echancrée'.*

BELOW: *Some rongorongo-script characters from the Santiago Staff.*

115

then adopted a method of 'script' that used motifs they had already been using in their rich rock art – the birds, fishes, turtles, vulvas, and other motifs in the rock art inventory also form part of the inscriptions. The signs were first lightly etched on the wood with sharp flakes of obsidian (volcanic glass) to provide an outline, and then deeply incised with a dull shark's tooth.

The script now survives only as markings on twenty-five pieces of wood – in pre-missionary days they were often destroyed in wars or deliberately burned, others were buried with the honoured dead, and it is possible that many were hidden in sacred caves to protect these symbols of paganism after the arrival of Christianity on the island. The known specimens, all housed in museums, contain a total of over 14,000 glyphs (or hieroglyphs) – ranging from one artefact with only two glyphs incised on it, to 2,300 on another. The island's *rongorongo* experts escaped the slave raids of 1862/3 which took numerous islanders off to Peru, but they died in the subsequent smallpox epidemic, and this is why the tablets' content has largely remained a mystery.

A major breakthrough in cracking the *rongorongo* code was recently achieved by Steven Fischer, a specialist in linguistics and epigraphy. The 'Rosetta Stone' in his decipherment was the Santiago Staff, a 2-kilogram wooden sceptre acquired by Chileans in 1870; measuring 126 centimetres by 6.5 centimetres, it once belonged to an Easter Island *ariki* or leader. Fischer discovered that this staff, uniquely among *rongorongo* inscriptions, marks textual divisions with about ninety-seven irregularly spaced vertical lines; and he also noticed that each glyph that starts a new division (i.e. is immediately to the right of a vertical line) is suffixed with a phallus-like motif; and in the series of glyphs within each division, almost every third one (the fourth, seventh, tenth, thirteenth, etc.) also has this phallic suffix. Not one division has the suffix on its last or its penultimate glyph; not one division contains fewer than three glyphs; most divisions comprise multiples of three, and the first in each trio sports a huge phallus in almost every case. In other words, the Santiago Staff has a basic triad structure, which also seems to occur on some other *rongorongo* artefacts. Based on a recitation by an old islander in 1886, and on our knowledge of ancient

Polynesian beliefs, Fischer has concluded that the *rongorongo* inscriptions on which he has detected the triad structure are cosmogonies (creation chants) – a whole succession of copulations (each triad denoting that X copulated with Y and the result was Z) to explain the creation of everything in the world. Among the other inscriptions, one appears to be a calendar text of some sort, as was discovered in the 1950s, and then there are anomalous groupings of signs that still have to be identified as to genre. The *rongorongo* script still retains much of its mystery.

What Happened to Easter Island

It is impossible now to know exactly what happened on Easter Island. However, the probably steady growth of the population together with the decline in food and increased importance of economically useless activities (platform building, statue carving and transportation) seem to have led to a collapse.

The causes of the island's decline and change were probably complex – it is possible that the climatic episode known as the 'Little Ice Age' may have played a role – but even the far greater climatic changes of the earlier Ice Age proper did not have an impact anything like the arrival of humans. The major factor in the island's collapse was clearly the human colonization. Pollen analysis has revealed here the most dramatic deforestation known in the archaeological record. From at least 1,200 years ago one can see a massive reduction in forest cover until, by the time Europeans arrived, there were no large trees left. The imported rats fed on the palm fruits and helped prevent regenerations. Without the palm and other timber, statues could no longer be moved (hence the abandonment of work in the quarry); ocean-going canoes could no longer be built, thus cutting the population off from the crucial protein supply of deep-sea fish; and deforestation also caused massive soil erosion which damaged crop-growing potential. Chickens became the most precious source of protein, guarded like treasure in fortified structures. Starvation gave rise to raiding and violence, and perhaps even to cannibalism.

By 1722, when Europeans arrived, it was virtually over. The population had been reduced to about 2,000 people, living in poverty amid the ruins of

their former culture. The palm tree and several other species became extinct, leaving the island with only one small species of tree and two of shrubs. Subsequent slave raids and epidemics eventually reduced the population to just over one hundred, wiping out almost all of the ruling and priestly clans who could have revealed so much of the island's culture, and of its *rongorongo*. Instead we have had to build up a picture from the stunted testimony of the descendants of these few survivors, from archaeological and palaeo-environmental investigations and from experimentation. Our knowledge of what happened on Easter Island is far from perfect, and will certainly change as more evidence comes to light. But at least we have a clear idea of the unimaginable cultural achievements and ingenuity, as well as the environmental shortsightedness, of that unique island's remarkable population.

View out of the cave of Ana Kai Tangata (which means 'eat men cave' or perhaps 'cave that eats men' or 'cave where men eat'!), showing the wall paintings of terns.

CLOUD CITIES OF
THE INKA

KAREN WISE

The year is 1532. A group of fewer than 200 Spanish soldier-explorers, accompanied by a few Catholic priests, arrive on the north coast of what is now Peru. Disembarking, they begin a journey of discovery and destruction that will end in the downfall of an empire that covers much of western South America. In their quest for gold and glory, the Spanish colonists, or con-quistadores, take over the huge and efficient government of the Inka, changing the course not only of American but also of European history.

The great empire of the Inka had been built quickly, during the hundred years before the arrival of the Spanish. By the time of European contact, the Inka had annexed an area larger than even the great Roman empire. Even more amazing, the Inka empire covered some of the roughest terrain on earth, including desert, the steep mountains of the Andes range, and dense jungles. Without the wheel, and lacking any animal that could be ridden, the Inka were able to move huge numbers of men and resources quickly across vast expanses of varied lands. They amassed great wealth and kept strict accounts without writing as we know it. Where did this great empire come from? How was it ruled? And how could a few Spaniards conquer it so quickly?

The Origins of the Empire

The Inka empire emerged after thousands of years of cultural development in the Andes. The Inka harnessed technology, economic, social, political and religious practices that had grown from the deserts, mountains and even the jungles of South America to control vast territories and huge populations during the fifteenth and sixteenth centuries AD. The Inka modified everything from farming practices to religious rituals to suit their aims, and reinforced their legitimacy by re-telling history to emphasize their own civilization over those that had preceded them.

Characteristically, the Inka tale of their own origins emphasized Inka divine right as well as their civilizing influence on the surrounding peoples. One version of the Inka origin story was written by the Spanish colonial chronicler Bernabé Cobo in the early seventeenth century:

There came forth from a cave ... Pacarictampu ... four brothers called Manco Capac, Ayar Chache, Ayar Uchi and Agay Manco; and with them four sisters of theirs, who were called Mama Huaco, Mama Ocllo, Mama Ragua and Mama Cura ... With the seeds of maize and other foods that the Creator gave them, they set off on the road to the Valley of Cuzco ... They came to a high hill called the Hanacauri (which afterwards was a famous place of worship among the Indians because this fable took place there) and from there the eldest brother marked the land, and, hurling four slingstones towards the four corners of the

earth, he took possession of it . . . one of the brothers returned to Pacarictampu, entered the cave . . . and remained there without ever appearing again; of the three that remained, two of them turn themselves into stones . . . thus only Manco Capac arrived with his four sisters at the site where the city of Cuzco is located now. There Manco Capac made friends little by little with the natives of the region, who were few in number and lived spread out over that valley like savages without order or harmony. With the industry and help of his sisters, who called him the son of the Sun and spoke to him with great respect and reverence, especially because he was a peaceful, very prudent and humane man, he came to be respected and obeyed by all. (Cobo, *History of the Inca Empire* (Austin, 1979), pp. 103–4)

This was one of the stories the Inka told about

themselves. Other evidence, especially from archaeological studies, indicates that the Inka were in no way responsible for bringing either agriculture or civilization to the Andes, although they may eventually have brought relative peace to the Cuzco region. Before their emergence as rulers of an empire, the Inka were the inhabitants of one of many small competing and warlike cities found in the area beginning in the eleventh century. Far from civilizing savage peoples, the Inka fought with, and finally conquered, nearby cities inhabited by people much like themselves. They went on, however, to conquer vast territories, and by the mid-sixteenth century had annexed an area that stretched from modern-day Colombia to Chile, and from the desert coast on the west well into the jungles east of the Andean mountain chain. Without horses, the wheel, or writing as we know it, the Inka conquered a territory larger than any then known on earth,

View of the Inka ruins of Machu Picchu, one of the most famous archaeological sites in the New World. The beauty, setting and aura of mystery surrounding the site continue to fascinate visitors from around the world.

119

developing a vast economy that was efficient at both feeding people and transporting goods.

Cuzco, the Inka Capital

The imperial city of Cuzco was both the heart and the head of the Inka empire. Located at 3,395 metres above sea level, Cuzco is one of the highest capital cities known. Carefully planned and constructed, Cuzco featured a huge central plaza that was surrounded by massive buildings. The city was laid out along a grid pattern (some say in the shape of a puma), and its 4,000 buildings were found in two major sectors, known as upper and lower Cuzco. Inka Cuzco was a splendid city, and many of its buildings were built of cut and dressed stone that was fitted together so precisely that no mortar was needed. The walls of many of the important buildings were painted and some were finished with gold and silver.

In Inka geography, Cuzco was the hub of the empire, with both secular and sacred lines and roads leading out from its centre. The empire was known as Tawantinsuyu, or the Land of the Four Quarters, and the kingdom was divided into four sections for administrative purposes. Each of the four quarters had a governor. Inka administration was hierarchical, with local leaders at the base and a series of administrators overseeing the local leaders, particularly ensuring that each group provided the Inka with the labour and goods they owed to the Inka.

The task of keeping track of the goods that flowed in and out of Inka storehouses and of all other aspects of Inka activities was a huge job. It is hard to understand how the Inka managed it without a system of writing (symbolic representation of spoken language). What they did have was an extraordinary method of record-keeping using groups of knotted string, known as *quipu*, which were made and read by trained specialists. *Quipu* were made of long cords of coloured string, and knots and groups of knots placed at specific intervals represented numbers in the decimal system. Because the *quipu* are so different from European writing, most of the Spanish do not seem to have recognized them for what they were, native records of the empire, and many were destroyed. Those that remain in museums around the world continue to intrigue researchers, who try to understand how this system, so different from our own, was used.

LEFT: *A kero (or ceremonial vase) depicting an Inka nobleman (orejon) in a cape and feather headdress. Depictions on pottery and other artefacts help archaeologists reconstruct ancient patterns of dress and behaviour.*

Transportation was critical in the ancient empire, just as it is today. The Inka built a huge network of roads that ran the length and width of the empire, linking Cuzco with major and minor regional capitals, administrative centres, outposts and religious pilgrimage sites. The Inka road system covered more than 25,000 kilometres, and perhaps as much as 40,000 kilometres. Road construction varied, depending on terrain, and could include huge stone stairways and long bridges where necessary. On important roads, way-stations that included storehouses for food and other important state resources were found about a day's walk from one another. The wheel was not used by the Inka, and they had no animal such as the horse that could be ridden; they did, however, have the llama, a small South American relative of the camel that was used as a pack animal as well as for meat. Huge caravans of llamas carried goods across the empire. In addition, runners, known as *chaski*, could wait at way-stations along the Inka roads, from which they ran relay-style to deliver messages and even goods to the Inka.

OPPOSITE: *The Inkas combined stone carving, masonry and natural rock in settings such as Machu Picchu.*

century. They developed a sumptuary code, including rules prohibiting all but the Inka royalty from wearing certain clothing and symbols, and limiting the use of many titles to descendants of the original Inka towns. The Inka eventually allowed the people from towns surrounding Cuzco to use special titles and wear certain clothes previously limited to the Inka, but they enforced strictly the divisions between people of different towns and regions, as well as different classes.

The Inka first conquered the nearby groups, building a base of power in the Cuzco area over the course of several generations. Then, during the second half of the fifteenth century, a vast expansion took place, accompanied by military campaigns and incredible logistical feats. The army was marched huge distances to conquer areas ever further from Cuzco. The soldiers walked, accompanied by huge caravans of llamas, packing provisions as well as porters and other support personnel. The armies were fed from what they brought and were also provided for from the vast stores kept in provincial capitals and at roadside way-stations.

As the empire grew, so too did the wealth and power of the Inka. The state used a variety of mechanisms to build infrastructure and to establish itself in each new region that was conquered. When they subdued small states and chiefdoms, they took over the capitals and made them into regional administrative centres. In areas that lacked adequate infrastructure for the needs of the empire, the Inka constructed new provincial capitals, centralizing regional power. They often constructed new agricultural canals and terraces, modifying and expanding existing productive networks, and installing state storehouses and administrative centres.

Whenever possible, the Inka used the local kings and chiefs to help them take over new regions. If the local rulers co-operated, they received wealth and privilege and were allowed to maintain and even enhance their political power within the local region. Of course, not all local leaders were content to serve the growing Inka state, and those who preferred independence were removed and sometimes dealt with harshly. To prevent rebellion by local leaders, the Inka developed systems of incentives and punishments. The sons of local leaders

The Inka built wide roads across the desert, narrow stairways and paths through mountain passes, and suspension bridges across impassable sections of torrential rivers, like this one, which crossed the Apurimac River in the highlands of Peru, drawn by E. G. Squier.

How the Inka Conquered the Andes

Pre-Inka Peru was dominated by many small local states, as well as by a few larger and more important regional states, such as the Chimu empire on the north coast of Peru. As the Inka came to rule the areas around Cuzco in the early fifteenth century, they began to develop some of the traits that would characterize them as the empire grew. Distinctive pottery and clothing were developed and the Inka began to codify the rules and customs that were to dominate the Andean world for the next

were taken to Cuzco to be educated in the Inka system. This had two advantages: the young heirs to local leaders would be educated to take over rule of their homelands in the style that best suited the Inka; furthermore, the young heirs kept in Cuzco

another and were likely to report on any illegal activities by their neighbours. Groups of people who were moved by the Inka, especially those who were loyal to the Inka, were often placed in areas of either strategic or economic importance, where

A gold votive figure of a llama. Metalworking in gold, silver and copper was practised throughout the Inka empire. During the early colonial period the Spanish collected as much gold and silver as they could find and shipped it to Spain, and few artefacts such as this one survive.

served as potential hostages in case their fathers or other relatives staged a rebellion against the state.

Local groups who proved especially difficult to subdue were dealt with largely through removal. Although local rebellious leaders might be executed or otherwise punished, their followers would simply be moved to other areas. In the most extreme cases, part or all of a village population was moved from its homes, and replaced with other groups more loyal to the state. People from different towns and regions were suspicious of one

they could develop new areas of agricultural productivity and keep watch on less loyal local people.

The Inka built up vast wealth by deploying and developing traditional patterns of community-based labour. Although they exacted tribute in the form of raw materials and finished goods from some areas and in certain circumstances, most of the state's resources were gathered through what is often called a labour tax. Under the most common system, communities provided the state with labour, and each able-bodied male member of the community spent a certain percentage of his time working directly for the state. State-owned agricultural fields and flocks of animals were cared for by members of each local community. The subjects of the Inka also made cloth for the empire, and worked on state projects, including road and bridge building, and the construction of large buildings. While they worked on state or communal projects, the people were provided with food and with *chicha* beer and coca leaves, and larger projects would be done in a festival atmosphere.

In addition to those who worked part time for the state under the labour tax system, there were also groups of both men and women who worked full time for the state, and who were fed and clothed by the state. The best-known group was that of the women known as *mamakuna*. Beautiful young girls from around the kingdom were taken from their homes to live apart in groups of other such women. The *mamakuna* wove cloth, brewed *chicha*, and engaged in religious activities. The Inka controlled the rights to marriage and reproduction of these women, who could be given by the Inka either in marriage or as concubines to favoured kinsmen and regional leaders. There were also men who worked full time for the Inka, mostly as herders, but they could marry as they chose and only their herding activities seem to have been controlled by the state.

Agriculture was one of the mainstays of the

Inka economy, and it was intensified and expanded in many areas. Land was divided in a three-tiered system. Local communities controlled much of it, and on these lands most people grew the crops that fed them and their families. There were also lands dedicated to certain religious shrines, cults and rituals, where community members grew crops and herded animals that were used to support religious activities. State lands were those owned by the Inka, and worked by local people under the labour tax system. From these lands came the stores of food, wool, animals and other goods amassed by the state and kept in state warehouses until needed to support military campaigns or other state needs.

Religion and Sacrifice

Inka religion was based on allegiance not just to the sun, father of the Inka, but also to moon, stars and earth, as well as to innumerable gods and spirits who inhabited mountains, streams, rocks and other natural features. The gods of the Inka were worshipped in every setting, from the spectacular and monumental Temple of the Sun in Cuzco to tiny shrines found across the empire. Worship included many forms of offerings and sacrifices. Offerings often included such things as *chicha* and coca leaves, as well as items of food and small carved figures. Animals, including domesticated guinea pigs, llamas and alpacas, were also sacri-

The intiwatana, often called the 'Hitching Post of the Sun', may have been used to observe movements of the sun, or for sacrifices and ceremonies.

ficed, especially at major ceremonies. In some cases, human sacrifices also took place.

Although human sacrifice was not common it was important, and major ceremonies were held when it occurred. A recent archaeological discovery of a young girl who was sacrificed on a high peak in southern Peru provides some indication of what happened. The girl, a teenager, was fed and drugged, led up a sacred mountain, and there killed with a blow to the head. She was wrapped in fine cloth and her body left as an offering, possibly to the thunder god.

The Conquest

One of the most often asked questions about the demise of the Inka empire is how could it have been possible for less than 200 Spanish adventurer-soldiers, many of them illiterate opportunists, to have conquered this powerful empire. The best answer seems to be a combination of luck, disease and technology. In the first place, the Inka seem not to have had a well-established system for succession. They generally had many children, one of whom would be designated as the heir. At the time

the Spanish arrived the Inka ruler Huayna Capac had died, as had his designated heir. Another son, Atahualpa, had been fighting for the throne. With his brother dead, possibly of smallpox, which the Europeans had just introduced to the vulnerable natives, Atahualpa seemed destined to take over as the Inka ruler. The Spanish, however, succeeded in capturing Atahualpa, holding him for a huge ransom of gold and silver, and then killing him.

The Spanish were able to ally themselves with some of the groups that opposed Atahualpa, as well as with other groups who had not been happy under the Inka, and who saw the Spaniards as their chance to escape from the yoke of Inka rule. The Spanish also had guns, which, though slow to load and far less accurate than the bows and spears of the Inka warriors, were novel and certainly loud. Horses, too, may have proved daunting to the natives. It seems most likely, however, that the combination of European diseases, and the circumstances within the young empire itself, provided the most important support for the bands of Spaniards who took over an empire and established what would be hundreds of years of colonial rule.

The city of Ollantaytambo in Cuzco province, one of the last to be built by the Inkas.

125

MYTHS
&
LEGENDS?

LOST ATLANTIS

THE ALCHEMISTS

THE HOLY SHROUD

THE HOLY GRAIL

THE KNIGHTS TEMPLAR

LOST ATLANTIS

JENNIFER WESTWOOD

Plato (circa 427– 347 BC), the Greek philosopher whose account of Atlantis is the only independent source for the story (Paris, Louvre).

A great imperial power destroyed by a cataclysm, an island sunk beneath the sea: this is the tragedy of Atlantis. Is the story true, and if so where was the lost island? Classical scholars, mythologists, archaeologists, historians, anthropologists, geophysicists, science-fiction writers, occultists (and others) have all had their ideas, coloured by their own preoccupations. So far, no location suggested has stood the test of time, each generation dismantling the arguments of the last in search of its own answers.

The story

Let us begin at the beginning, with two 'dialogues' composed by the Greek philosopher Plato a little more than 2,300 years ago. They are imaginary conversations between Socrates (before 469–399 BC) and three friends, and they are called after their main speakers *Timaeus* and *Critias*.

In them, Critias, Plato's maternal great-grandfather, tells a story he heard as a child from *his* grandfather, Critias the Elder (d. 403 BC), then a man of nearly ninety. The elder Critias himself heard it from his father, Dropides, who heard it from his friend, the great Athenian law-giver Solon (*circa* 640– *circa* 559 BC). Solon said he was told it by an aged priest at the temple of Sais, Egypt, where it was preserved in ancient records.

This story, apparently handed down in Plato's

128

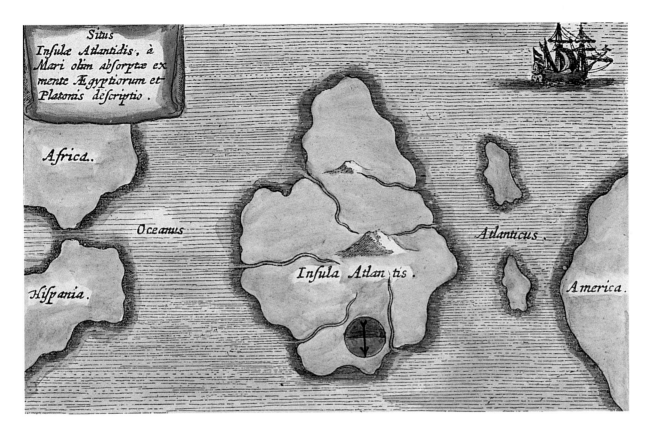

The island of Atlantis, outside the Pillars of Heracles. From Athanasius Kircher's Mundus Subterraneus *(1678).*

own family, is the tale of how ancient Athens had checked a mighty power which 9,000 years before had launched an attack on the cities of Europe and Asia from its base in the Atlantic:

There was an island opposite the strait which you call . . . the Pillars of Heracles, an island larger than Libya and Asia combined . . . On this island of Atlantis had arisen a powerful and remarkable dynasty of kings, who . . . controlled, within the strait, Libya up to Egypt and Europe as far as Tyrrhenia [Italy]. This dynasty . . . attempted to enslave at a single stroke . . . all the territory within the straight.

Athens led an alliance of the Greeks against the invaders, and when they deserted her fought on alone. Victorious, the Athenians liberated those who had fallen under the Atlantean yoke.

At a later time there were earthquakes and floods of extraordinary violence, and in a single dreadful day and night . . . the island of Atlantis . . . was swallowed up by the sea and vanished; this is why the sea in that area is to this day impassable to navigation, which is hindered by mud just below the surface, the remains of the sunken island . . .

In the *Critias*, after describing ancient Athens, Critias recounts the origins of the Atlanteans, descendants of Poseidon, god of the sea and earthquakes, and gives an account of their mountainous but fertile island, rich in timber, minerals and animals, including 'numerous elephants'.

He describes their extraordinary capital city, built around an acropolis, on which stood their palace, in the middle of which, surrounded by a golden wall, was Poseidon's temple, huge and 'somewhat outlandish'. Hot and cold springs fed open pools and covered hot baths for winter use, with separate arrangements for kings, commoners, women, horses and other beasts of burden.

The acropolis was defended by five concentric rings of alternating water and land, connected by bridges and tunnels. The two land rings held temples and gardens, exercise grounds and a racecourse. The three water rings, linked to the sea by a wide canal, enabled ships to sail into the heart of the city.

The ten kings of Atlantis were descendants of five pairs of twins, all sons, born by the mortal Cleito to Poseidon. They ruled under the suzerainty of the house of Atlas, the eldest, from whom Atlantis took its name. Every fifth or sixth year they assembled for consultation in Poseidon's temple; before deliberations began, the kings, armed with clubs and nooses, hunted the sacred bulls roaming at large there, and sacrificed one to Poseidon.

After many generations the Atlanteans degenerated from a noble super-race into greedy aggressors. Almighty Zeus decided to punish them and called an assembly of the gods. At this point Critias's narrative breaks off. The dialogue was left unfinished.

Atlantis-in-the-Atlantic

Argument over whether Plato's lost paradise was ever a real place began within fifty years of his death in 348/7 BC. His pupil Aristotle thought it was a political fable. By the time Pliny the Elder came to write his *Natural History* (AD 77) opinion was divided into two camps: believers and sceptics.

But, if a fact, where was it? Accepting Plato's description of it as lying opposite the 'Pillars of Heracles', which in the ancient world normally meant the Straits of Gibraltar, it was in the Atlantic. From the first this lent the story great mystique. The ancient Greeks envisaged the Atlantic as part of the ocean which encircled the world, and though the adventurous Carthaginians had sailed through the Pillars of Heracles, and up and down the coast, the Greeks knew little of it, believing it unnavigable.

To the Roman historian Tacitus, writing in AD 98, the Atlantic was still the 'unknown sea'. This reputation is precisely why many other mysterious, paradisal islands were located in it – the Fortunate Isles, the Island of the Seven Cities,

Maida, St Brendan's Isle, Hy Breasil. They were long marked on maps and sought on voyages of discovery – Hy Breasil was only dropped from mariners' charts in 1865.

Meantime, in 1553, about fifty years after Columbus discovered America, the Spanish historian Francesco López de Gómara pointed out that the West Indies and the American continent pretty well matched Plato's account of a 'continent' lying beyond Atlantis. Thereafter, that Atlantis was in the New World found many advocates, not least Francis Bacon in his utopian *Nova Atlantis* (1614–18).

The idea of America as Atlantis faded as more was learned of the New World, but Atlantis continued to be placed in the Atlantic. Athanasius Kircher, in *Mundus Subterraneus* (1655), suggested that the Azores were the mountain peaks of the sunken land; others pointed to the Madeiras and Canaries.

The most influential advocate of Atlantis-in-the-Atlantic was the American writer Ignatius Donnelly (1831–1901), who in 1882 published *Atlantis: The Antediluvian World*. Plato's Atlantis, 'larger than Asia and Libya' (Asia Minor and North Africa) amounts to a sizable land-mass. Following Kircher, Donnelly proposed that this drowned 'continent' was represented by the Azores, the volcanic tops of a structure called the Mid-Atlantic Ridge, discovered in the 1870s, that runs roughly north to south down the centre of the Atlantic Basin.

At the time, Donnelly's ideas seemed to have at least some scientific basis, but his case was destroyed by discoveries made in the 1960s supporting the theory of 'plate tectonics'. Briefly, most earth scientists now accept that the crust forming the Atlantic ocean floor was never continent-building material; and that the volcanic peaks along the Mid-Atlantic Ridge, rather than being relics of a sunken continent, are comparatively young. As far as science is concerned, the spectre of a submerged continent in the Atlantic has been laid to rest.

Occult Atlantis

This may not be quite the end of it, though. The Atlantic was also a favourite location for psychics and occultists drawn to Atlantean studies in the nineteenth and twentieth centuries. Using clairvoyance, psychic intuition, hypnotic regression to former lives and the 'Akashic Records', a history of

RIGHT: *The so-called Cross of Atlantis, a symbolic representation of the acropolis ringed by land and water described by Plato.*

all past events said by Rudolf Steiner (1861–1925) to exist on the astral plane, occultists claimed that Atlantis existed in an almost unbelievably ancient past – long before scientists place the first appearance of man on the planet – and that it was the source of a secret wisdom.

This brings us to Atlantology – as Atlantis-hunting has come to be known. The term is often used to imply a certain dottiness by sober scholars perturbed at the claims made by some Atlantologists in defence of their theories, as when Frank Joseph in *Atlantis in Wisconsin* (1995) argues that the reason other divers have not seen the structures he reports is because they shift into another dimension. A degree of obsessiveness attaches to the subject and fraud is not unknown: Paul Schliemann, grandson of Heinrich Schliemann, the discoverer of Troy, in 1912 claimed to have learned from his grandfather of a bowl he found at Troy, inscribed 'From King Chronos of Atlantis'. This bowl proved to be a fake when examined.

Wishful thinking is exceedingly common. Excitement was great in the late 1960s over the so-called 'Bimini Road', a J-shaped configuration of stones lying about 6 metres underwater off the coast of North Bimini, Bahamas, sighted in 1968 and hailed as an ancient man-made pavement. Along with a building alleged to be a pre-Columbian temple, found a year earlier off Andros, it was said to confirm predictions made by the American medium Edgar Cayce (1877–1945), concerning the reappearance of Atlantis: 'expect it in 1968 or 1969.' As it turned out, the 'temple' was a sponge store built in the 1930s, and in 1981 the US Geological Survey produced conclusive evidence that the 'Bimini' Road was laid down by natural means a mere 2,500–3,500 years ago.

Diving for Atlantis around the Atlantic will doubtless continue in the teeth of the evidence, because what fuels the quest is romance. For centuries, legends of 'sunken cities' have existed along the Atlantic coast, many of them based on occasional glimpses by fishermen and other seafarers of what look like sunken 'roads' and 'walls'. In addition, great discoveries in underwater archaeology, such as the remains of the Pharos Lighthouse, one of the seven wonders of the world, in Alexandria harbour in the mid-1990s, lure amateur archaeologists on.

Mayan vase, Tikal, Guatemala. The anthropologist Lewis Spence (1874–1955) thought the Mayans belong to an Atlantean 'culture-complex' embracing Central America, North Africa and Spain.

The Mediterranean Solution

Many Atlantis-seekers have ignored Plato's statement that the Atlantean power was based in the Atlantic. The seventeenth-century Swedish scholar Olaüs Rudbeck located Atlantis in Sweden. In 1762 Frederick Baër equated the ten Atlantean kingdoms with the *twelve* tribes of Israel and the Atlantic with the Red Sea. The eighteenth-century French astronomer Jean Bailly placed the lost island off Spitsbergen. By the late nineteenth century, it had also been discovered in the Sahara, the Caucasus, South Africa, Ceylon, Brazil, Greenland, the British Isles, Prussia and the Netherlands. Rand and Rose Flem-Ath in *When the Sky Fell* (1995) make a case for Antarctica.

The ancient Greeks applied the name 'Pillars of Heracles' not only to the Straits of Gibraltar, but also to the narrow Straits of the Dardanelles, the entrance to the Black Sea. This has encouraged searchers for Atlantis to look within the Mediterranean world.

In 1900, the archaeologist Sir Arthur Evans discovered the Palace of Knossos on Crete, and dubbed the prehistoric civilization he found there 'Minoan'. In February 1909 an anonymous article appeared in *The Times* under the heading 'The Lost Continent', which suggested that in Minoan Crete Evans had also found Atlantis. Later the writer, K. T. Frost, argued his case more fully. He proposed that the story of Atlantis was an Egyptian memory of Bronze Age Crete, which in the first half of the second millennium BC had dominated the Aegean. He pointed to parallels between Plato's account and Minoan culture, not least that between the Atlantean kings' bull hunt and the bull-cult of Crete evidenced by the Greek legend of Theseus and the Minotaur, and by discoveries at Knossos. Unlike Atlantis, Crete had not sunk under the sea, so instead Frost suggested that the legend of Theseus preserved the memory of a Mycenaean invasion in about 1450 or 1400 BC that overthrew Cretan civilization.

Frost's theory was remembered by the Greek archaeologist Spyridon Marinatos, when, during excavations in the 1930s on the northern coast of Crete, he found both Minoan remains and quantities of pumice. Only 96 kilometres off was the arc-shaped volcanic island of Thera (modern

Santorini), and Marinatos knew its volcano had erupted in the Bronze Age. In 1939, he proposed that the collapse of Cretan power in the fifteenth century BC, indicated by the destruction of Knossos and other Minoan cities, was the result of a massive eruption of Thera, resulting in ash-falls and gigantic tidal waves. Returning to Frost's idea of a Minoan Atlantis he began in 1967 to excavate a site near Akrotiri in the south of Thera. He found a great prehistoric city with streets of houses, some still three storeys high, with rooms painted with exquisite frescoes. There were remains of furniture and fine pottery in a style which seemed to show that the city was both contemporary and probably linked with the Minoan palaces of Crete.

Marinatos and others painted a compelling picture of a prosperous commercial centre of the Minoan civilization which in about 1520 BC was overtaken by disaster. The Theran volcano erupted three times, the third time with such a crack that it may have been heard 3,000 kilometres away (estimates make the eruption four times as powerful as that of Krakatoa in 1883, which was heard in Australia). The volcano blanketed the island with ash, in some places 30 metres thick, burying the main city completely. About forty years later, the volcano's cone collapsed, creating tidal waves which destroyed Cretan civilization.

This dramatic scenario provided both an explanation of the fate of Crete and an original for Atlantis. The Crete-Thera solution became widely accepted, but twenty years on is losing support, not the least difficulty being that Theran ash discovered at other sites on Crete and in the Aegean seems to prove that Thera was destroyed by a single eruption anything up to 150 years earlier than the destruction of the Cretan palaces.

Shifting the setting closer to the Dardanelles, the geo-archaeologist Bernhard Zangger has since argued in *The Flood from Heaven* (1993) that the tale of Atlantis is an Egyptian version of the Trojan War. Peter James in *The Sunken Kingdom* (1995) similarly looks to modern Turkey for the solution, suggesting that Atlantis is an echo of what Pliny called 'the very celebrated city . . . that used to be called Tantalis'. According to Pliny it was destroyed by an earthquake and in his time lay under the 'marsh of Sale'. Pausanias (second century AD), author of the first guide to Greece, tells a local tale of what seems

The 'Lady of Elche' (fifth century BC), found at Elche, near Alicante, Spain, once hailed as an Atlantean priestess (Madrid, Archaeological Museum).

135

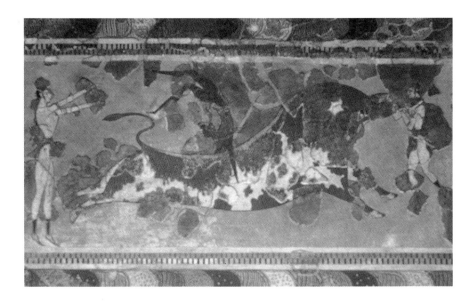

ABOVE: *The royal bull hunt of Atlantis has echoes of the ceremonial bull game depicted in a Minoan fresco at Knossos.*

OPPOSITE: *Solon (circa 640–559 BC), Athenian law-giver who, according to Plato, brought the story of Atlantis back from Egypt. Justus van Ghent, circa 1476.*

to be the same city, on Mount Sipylus (modern Manisa Dagi): 'it disappeared into a chasm, and from the fissure in the mountain water gushed forth, and the chasm became named Lake Saloe. The ruins of the city could still be seen in the lake until the water of the torrent covered them up.'

Fact or Fiction?

Plato is the only independent source for the story of Atlantis: everyone else who mentions it derives it from him. For all the theories and excavations, we are no nearer knowing for certain whether or not he made it up.

Some argue that Solon really *did* bring the story back from Egypt. There is nothing inherently impossible in the long chain of oral transmission from Solon to the younger Critias. Advocates of an Egyptian origin point to the similarity of the tale to one known in Egypt during the Middle Kingdom (2000–1750 BC). This is 'The Shipwrecked Traveller', which tells of a man who, after being shipwrecked, was cast up on a paradisal island, where he met a golden dragon. The dragon foretells that the Egyptian will be rescued, but 'never more shall you see this island because it will be swallowed by the waves'.

But if the story of Atlantis was remembered at Sais, as Plato says, why didn't the priests there also tell it to the historian Herodotus (*circa* 454–20 BC), who like Solon visited and talked with them? And would a story that came in its entirety from Egypt contain so much accurate knowledge of prehistoric

Athens? For Plato's account is as much about Athens as about Atlantis. He describes a circuit wall on top of the Acropolis, warriors' houses on its northern side, a spring on its top subsequently choked by earthquakes – Mycenaean features all confirmed by archaeology.

These are just a handful of the questions raised by Plato's text. Classical scholars on the whole share Aristotle's view that the story is a moral fable, a composite of ideas, historical facts, and ancient myths of the Golden Age and the Universal Deluge, made by Plato, who wished to explore further the ideal state he had outlined in *The Republic*. They point out that the Atlantis story mirrors the history of the Peloponnesian War (431–404 BC), waged by an Athens that, in the opinion of many of Plato's contemporaries, had no sooner overthrown the Persian Empire than it started empire-building of its own. By a reversal of roles, Atlantis represents the Athens of Plato's time, fallen from greatness; whilst the Athens of his tale is a combination of Sparta, the Athens of Mycenaean days, and the ideal society proposed in *The Republic*. A tantalizing footnote to this reading of the story – remembering that in Plato's account the Athenian army was destroyed during the cataclysm that overwhelmed Atlantis – is that in 426 BC, during the Peloponnesian War, a tidal wave wrecked an Athenian fortress on a little island off Locris, in central Greece. Its name was Atalante.

Even if Plato wove the story of Atlantis from an assortment of materials, this is not to say that the whole thing is fiction. And many, perhaps most, people *want* Atlantis to be true. We want our shrinking planet still to contain wonders. We want the promise of great adventures. It is a dull dog indeed who does not thrill to Verne's account in *Twenty Thousand Leagues Under the Sea* (1869) of Arronax's walk with Captain Nemo on the sea-bottom:

There were vast heaps of stone . . . There . . . under my eyes, ruined, destroyed, lay a town – its roofs open to the sky . . . Further on, some remains of a giant aqueduct . . . there traces of a quay . . . Further on again, long lines of sunken walls and broad, deserted streets . . . Where was I? Where was I? . . . Captain Nemo . . . picking up a piece of chalk . . . advanced to a rock . . . and traced the one word:

ATLANTIS.

THE
ALCHEMISTS

ROBERT JACKSON

They were a strange and secretive brotherhood. They believed that they could obtain untold wealth by changing base metals such as lead and copper into silver and gold, and they embarked on a quest to discover a mysterious substance called the Elixir of Life, which they thought could prolong human existence.

The Beginnings of Alchemy

They were the alchemists. They flourished throughout Europe in the Middle Ages, but the mystical science they practised – alchemy – is much older than that. It dates back at least 2,000 years to the days of ancient Greece. In fact, the word 'alchemy' comes originally from the Greek *chumeia*, which means the art of casting metals.

The early alchemists carried out many of their experiments in Alexandria, which in ancient times was a major centre of culture and learning. It was there that the Greek *chumeia* became the Arabic *al-kimiya*, from which the modern 'alchemy' is derived. But alchemy was also practised in China and India in ancient times. The first written evidence of Chinese alchemy dates back to 144 BC, when the emperor issued a proclamation warning that anyone using alchemical gold to mint coins would be put to death. In India, there are references to alchemy dating from around the second

century BC, but since Alexander the Great's expedition to India took place in 325 BC, it is possible that the Indians learned the principles from the Greeks.

Alchemists believed that they could change base metals into precious ones – a process called transmutation – with the aid of something called the 'philosopher's stone'. The principles behind this

The celebrated Pharos of Alexandria. Built in the reign of Ptolemy II, the lighthouse was one of the seven wonders of the ancient world.

theory were based on the ideas of the Greek philosopher Aristotle (384–322 BC), the tutor of Alexander the Great, who believed that everything in nature was subject to change. For example, seeds grow into grape vines, the grapes turn into wine, and wine turns into vinegar. So why, asked the alchemists, could lead and copper not be turned into silver and gold? All that was needed was a special substance to make it happen – the philosopher's stone.

The first alchemist we can identify by name is Bolos of Mendes, also known as Democritus, who lived in or near Alexandria in about 250 BC. He took his name from a Greek philosopher, Democritus

of Abdera, who had died over one hundred years earlier and who was the first person to form the theory that all matter was made of atoms.

Some of Democritus the alchemist's writings survive, and were discovered in Egypt in 1828. In them, he described various methods of making imitation gold. In one, the surface of another metal was coloured with a lacquer to make it look like gold, a process already well known in the world of ancient Greece.

Other early experiments were described in an encyclopedia of alchemy written by Zosimus around AD 300, parts of which have survived. Zosimus was a Greek historian, and his writings show that not all alchemists were men. A woman called Cleopatra was one (although she was not the famous Egyptian queen), and another was Maria the Jewess, a rather mysterious figure who invented several utensils which are still in use today. The *bain-marie*, a double pan for cooking sauces, is said to be named after her.

After the Roman conquest of Egypt the alchemists who had flourished in Alexandria and elsewhere were forced to go underground. The Romans were concerned that alchemical gold might be used to finance revolutionary factions, and when there was a rebellion in Egypt in AD 296 the Emperor Diocletian ordered the destruction of 290 manuscripts dealing with the manufacture of gold and silver by alchemical means.

The art of alchemy remained in the doldrums until AD 642, when the Arabs captured Alexandria from Byzantine rule. They soon became interested in alchemy themselves, and translated many works on the subject from Greek into Arabic.

The most important Arab alchemist during this period was Jabir ibn Hayyan, who was court alchemist to Harun al-Rashid, the caliph of *The Arabian Nights*. As well as practising alchemy, Jabir ibn Hayyan invented processes for the manufacture of acids which remained in use for many centuries.

Alchemy in Medieval Europe

In the eleventh and twelfth centuries alchemy found its way into western Europe with the crusaders returning from their battles against the forces of Islam. The first translation of an alchemical book from Arabic into Latin was made in 1144

by Robert of Chester, and the translated works of Jabir ibn Hayyan were eagerly read by medieval philosopher-scientists.

Suddenly, a new scientific fervour gripped Europe. Was it really possible, as the ancients claimed, to acquire enormous wealth by means of transmutation? The quest was on, and it was to last for centuries.

Opinion in the scientific world of medieval Europe – a world very much in the grip of superstition, myth and wild speculation – was divided. One of the leading thinkers of his time, Albertus Magnus (1193–1280) thought that it might be possible

ABOVE: *This medallion belonged to the seventeenth-century alchemist Wenzel Seiler. The bottom part was supposedly transmuted into gold by Seiler on 16 September 1677; in fact the gold had been overlaid with silver, which dissolved when the medallion was dipped in nitric acid.*

OPPOSITE: *An early sixteenth-century woodcut depicting alchemists at work.*

141

An alchemist's 'kitchen', or laboratory.

to create alchemical gold, but that it would be of inferior quality to pure gold. However, there was little open speculation about the techniques that might be used, simply because the practice of alchemy became a very secretive affair.

Many alchemists claimed to have achieved success, but not many were able to produce proof that their experiments had worked. One of the first was Nicholas Flamel (1330–1418), a notary at the University of Paris, who claimed to have dreamt about, and later found, a book containing the secrets of alchemy. With its aid, he succeeded in making the 'philosopher's stone', which he described as a red powder.

In 1392, he projected the powder on to half a pound of mercury, which was changed into the same quantity of silver. The experiment was witnessed only by his wife, but Flamel's contemporaries were inclined to believe his claim because of a sudden change in his circumstances. From having been a poor man he became quite wealthy, and donated money to several hospitals and churches in Paris.

Another man who believed that transmutation was possible was Jean-Baptiste van Helmont (1577–1644), a Flemish chemist and physician. Writing about the philosopher's stone, he said:

I have divers seen it and handled it with my hands, but it was of colour such as saffron in its powder, yet weighty and shining like unto powdered glass. There was once given unto me one fourth part of one grain. I projected it upon eight ounces of quicksilver [mercury] made hot in a crucible, and straightway all the quicksilver with a certain degree of noise stood still from flowing and being congealed settled like into a yellow lump; but after pouring it out, the bellows blowing, there were found eight ounces and a little less than eleven grains of the purest gold.

Other scientists believed that mercury was the key to transmutation. One was Sir Isaac Newton, known today as the 'father of modern physics', who spent many hours experimenting with it and suffered from mercury poisoning as a result. Newton's writings on alchemy amounted to some thousands upon thousands of pages, but they remain unpublished. (They were sold to private collectors in the 1930s.)

Some alchemists, however, believed that alchemy provided a foundation for serious scientific study. One was Philippus Paracelsus (1493–1541), a Swiss physician and alchemist who applied alchemical techniques to making medicines. He believed in transmutation, but his main concern was to prepare chemicals that would cure illness, rather than relying on traditional herbal remedies.

The Fraudulent Alchemists

Alchemy, naturally, was a fertile ground for fraud. One trickster was Simon Forman, who was born in 1552 and was imprisoned several times for false pretences. Having given up trying to make gold, he set about distilling love potions and strong drink, which was literally his downfall: his diaries record that he fell downstairs several times after a day's experimentation.

Some charlatans made a great deal of money through claiming to be able to manufacture gold. Domenico Caetano, an Italian who lived in the seventeenth century, persuaded the Elector of Bavaria to give him 60,000 florins – an enormous sum – so that he could set up an alchemical laboratory. When he failed to produce any gold, the Elector had him imprisoned, but he escaped after six years and turned up in Vienna, where he worked under an alias, the Count de Ruggiero. The Austrian Emperor Leopold employed him as the official court alchemist, and was considerate enough to die before Caetano was required to prove his claim.

The fraudster promptly offered his services to other European rulers, ending with King Frederick of Prussia. Like the others, Frederick parted with large sums of money, but he eventually saw through Caetano's confidence trick and had him hanged in 1709. Caetano was not the first alchemist to suffer the death penalty; Georg Honnauer was hanged in 1597 for failing to produce gold for the Prince of Württemberg, and Marie Ziegler was roasted alive for duping Duke Julius of Brunswick in 1575.

Queen Elizabeth I of England was not above being deceived; she employed an alchemist for two years before she sacked him. Another, John Dee, received a pension from Elizabeth on his return to England from Europe, where he had been operating with an accomplice, Edward Kelly. Their work

was financed by Rudolf II, the Holy Roman Emperor, who eventually saw them for what they were and had Kelly thrown into prison. Dee would probably have suffered a similar fate had Rudolf not gone mad in the meantime. It is fortunate for us that he was spared, as he produced some of the foundation-stones of modern mathematics.

Yet another fraudulent alchemist, James Price – a member of the prestigious Royal Society because of his genuine scientific achievements – claimed to have converted mercury into gold and silver seven times in his laboratory at Guildford, and published a paper about it in 1782. When the Royal Society put pressure on him to prove his claim, however, Price killed himself by drinking prussic acid – an admission of guilt if ever there was one.

One of the most delightful swindles concerned an Arabian alchemist, who set up business in Prague and invited the city's alchemists to witness a new process for multiplying gold. He would, he said, turn every 100 gold marks into 1,000. He duly invited twenty-four alchemists to his well-equipped laboratory, relieved them of 100 marks each and dropped the coins into a crucible. Then he placed another vessel, which he said contained various substances necessary for the experiment, inside a furnace.

A few minutes later, as the alchemists crowded round eagerly, the vessel exploded, filling the room with choking smoke. When it cleared, they found that the Arabian had vanished through a side window, along with their 2,400 gold marks.

The Mercury Connection

Throughout the history of alchemy, one thing stands out above all others: the alchemists' preoccupation with the heavy element, mercury. Quite apart from the fact that it resembled molten silver, serious alchemists believed that it possessed strange and mysterious powers.

Just how strange, modern science is slowly beginning to find out; but there is written evidence that ancient races knew far more about the extraordinary power of mercury than we of a modern age might think, and some of the most remarkable documentation comes from India.

Among the ancient Hindu sacred books we find the *Samarangana Sutradhara*, a collection of texts compiled in the eleventh century but probably drawing on much older source material. The *Samarangana* contains 230 stanzas that describe in detail the building of aerial craft, called *vimanas*, in ancient Indian legend. Part of the text reads:

Strong and durable must the body be made, like a great flying bird, of light material. Inside it one must place the mercury-engine with its iron heating apparatus underneath. By means of the power latent in the mercury which sets the driving whirlwind in motion a man sitting inside may travel a great distance in the sky in a most marvellous manner . . . Similarly, by using the prescribed process, one can build a vimana as large as the God-in-motion. Four strong mercury containers must be built into the interior structure. When these have been heated by fire from the iron containers, the vimana develops thunder-power through the mercury. And at once it becomes like a pearl in the sky.

If the alchemists of the seventeenth and eighteenth centuries knew of such documents it might explain their fascination with mercury as a substance of great and hidden power; and such knowledge there certainly was, for their experiments unfolded at a time when India was yielding her cultural secrets to foreign explorers and merchants.

The British nuclear physicist Edward Neville da Costa Andrade (1887–1971), who collected many of Sir Isaac Newton's early scientific papers, noted in a speech delivered at Cambridge University in 1946 that Newton knew something about the secret of mercury. Quoting Lord Atterbury, a contemporary of Newton, Andrade said:

Modesty teaches us to speak of the ancients with respect, especially when we are not familiar with their works. Newton, who knew them practically by heart, had the greatest respect for them, and considered them to be men of genius and superior intelligence who had carried their discoveries in every field much further than we today suspect, judging from what remains of their writings. More ancient writings have been lost than have been preserved, and perhaps our new discoveries are of less value than those that we have lost.

Quoting Newton, Andrade continued:

Because of the way by which mercury may be impregnated, it has been thought fit to be

Illustrations from the sixteenth-century alchemical work Splendor Solis, *said to have originated in Augsburg, Bavaria.*

14

VI   II   X

Ora
Lege Lege Lege Relege labora
et Invenies.

concealed by others that have known it, and therefore may be an inlet to something more noble, not to be communicated without immense danger to the world.

Immense danger to the world from mercury? What could that possibly mean?

The Modern Alchemists

In the early 1980s, rumours began to circulate that scientists had developed a strange and uniquely powerful explosive substance called 'red mercury'. At first its existence was considered to be a myth, but scientists today are taking it very seriously indeed. Not only is it something of immense power, it also has an application in nuclear-weapons' technology, and its existence could pose a serious threat to the world's attempts to stop the spread of nuclear weapons. Experts say that it could be used to make a baseball-sized neutron bomb.

Scientists think that red mercury is a compound of mercury and antimony, bound together in a nuclear reactor. The alchemists of old attempted the binding of mercury and antimony, but they lacked the necessary technology.

Is it possible, then, that today's scientists have stumbled on a secret known to certain ancient races – that the element mercury, treated in a certain fashion, possesses extraordinary powers? And were the more serious alchemists, like Sir Isaac Newton, attempting to rediscover these powers? If so, then the declared aim of transmuting base metals into gold was a secondary one. But the irony is that the transmutation of elements is possible today – with the aid of nuclear physics. Without knowing it, the alchemists were experimenting with the dawn of the nuclear age.

OPPOSITE: *A symbolic illustration from an alchemical work of 1702, showing the weighing and mixing of alchemical substances. The lower picture represents the conjunction of the sun and moon.*

RIGHT: *Alchemical symbolism: the 'Dove of the Spirit' descends to form a trinity with the 'Solar King' and 'Lunar Queen'. The imagery represents the mystic triangle.*

THE HOLY SHROUD

TRISTAN GRAY HULSE

On the night of 28 May 1898 Secondo Pia clambered up on to a specially constructed platform in front of the high altar of the cathedral in Turin. He had been asked to photograph a length of ancient closely woven linen exhibited in an elaborate frame above the altar. Using his cumbersome camera and relying on the usually less-than-reliable electric lights of the period, which had already defeated his attempts to photograph the cloth on 25 May, Pia slowly exposed two glass plates. Then he took the plates back to his studio to develop them.

The Shroud Rediscovered

For centuries, this ancient linen cloth, measuring approximately 4.5 x 1.1 metres, has been venerated as the actual burial shroud of Jesus Christ. The cloth shows, in a faint and shadowy way, the front and rear images of a dead man. These images are sepia-coloured, with reddish marks suggesting blood-stains at the wrists, feet and side of the dead man – the whole seemingly recording the impressions made when the body of a man executed in the most barbarous of manners was laid upon one half of the cloth, and the other half was folded over him. The supposed blood-stains basically conform to the accounts of the crucifixion of Jesus given in the Gospels.

It was this vague image which Signor Pia expected to see when he developed his plates. What he in fact saw created an immediate sensation and has generated controversy ever since, for Pia's negatives revealed, not the shadowy image on the Shroud itself, but a fully rounded and extraordinarily detailed portrait of the Man on the Shroud. Pia believed – and since then millions have shared his conviction – that he was gazing, for the first time in history, upon the actual face of Jesus.

The news, and the new images, rapidly spread across the world, and battle-lines were quickly formed, for and against the integrity of the Shroud as a real relic of Christ and the genuineness or otherwise of its astounding image. In France in 1902 Professor Yves Delage, himself an agnostic, scandalized the august French Academy by telling them that the Shroud was the true burial-cloth of Jesus.

At the same time the biologist Paul Vignon conducted researches which appeared to show that the images on the Shroud conformed exactly to the procedures of an actual crucifixion, and his iconographic studies demonstrated that the newly revealed face of Jesus was significantly similar to the images of Jesus accepted as such by the Church since earliest times. Vignon's subsequent books have been greatly influential. Also at this period, the Frenchman Ulysse Chevalier and the English Jesuit Herbert Thurston, both of them Catholic priests who based their work on medieval documentation of the Shroud, roundly condemned it as a forgery, the work of some medieval artist. To this day, scientific and historic interest in the Shroud is similarly polarized.

Since 1898, thousands of photographs have been taken of the Holy Shroud. Each one has clearly revealed, in photographic negative, an image of startling clarity and sophistication – an image, as so many have readily believed, that could not have been deliberately fabricated today, let alone by a medieval forger. Groups of experts assembled to try to decipher the riddle of the Shroud, but, following the tradition of centuries, the Holy Shroud was exposed to view only once or twice each hundred years, thus permitting few chances for proper investigation. An initial scientific examination was organized by the archbishop of Turin in 1969, and in 1973 the Swiss criminologist Max Frei took pollen samples from the surface of the cloth. From these, he was able to argue that the Shroud had indeed been in all the places it was known or might validly be suggested to have been in the years since the crucifixion and burial of Jesus. This seemed impressive, but in 1977 a conference of US scientists in Albuquerque, New Mexico, became the prelude to what was to be a seemingly much more conclusive series of tests.

In 1978 the Holy Shroud was removed from its shrine in the Royal Chapel of Turin Cathedral, and exhibited for veneration. Over six weeks, more than three million people came to see it. Afterwards, between 8 and 12 October, it was the object of intensive study by the US-based Shroud of Turin Research Project (STURP), when some twenty-five scientists subjected it to an extraordinary variety of tests. The team's photographer, Vernon Miller, took the most detailed and beauti-

ful series of photographs available to date. The findings were astounding. The sepia body-image was found to be entirely on the surface of the fabric, rather than absorbed into it; which meant that the image was formed in some way other than by simple contact with the bloody, sweat-soaked body of Jesus, as had previously been supposed. At the same time, the substance of the reddish stains was revealed as consonant with the chemical constituents of real blood.

To many, it seemed that the Shroud had finally

Giulio Clovio (1498–1578), The Holy Shroud of Turin.

The image of Jesus Christ as seen on the Shroud of Turin.

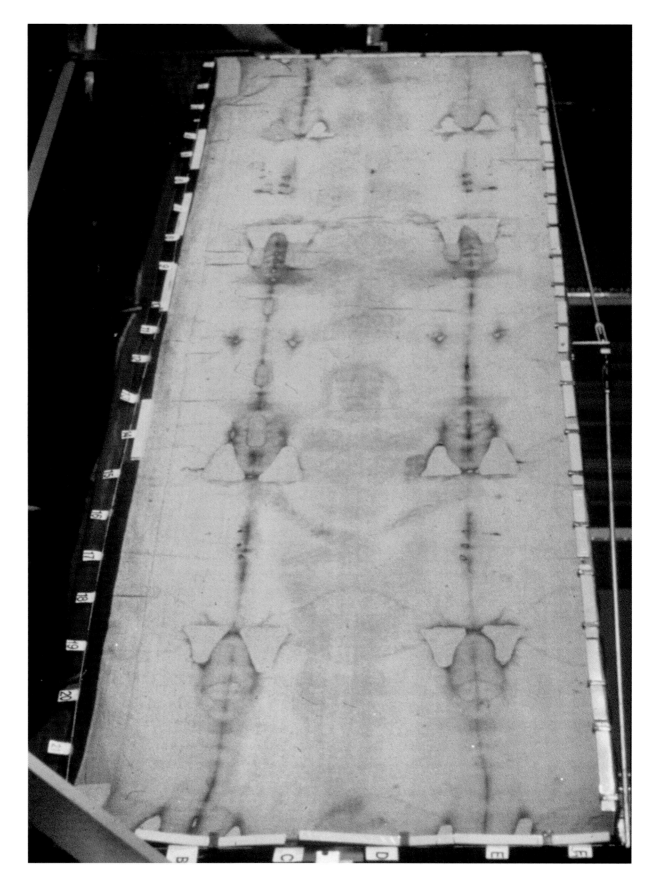

been vindicated. Speculation turned to the actual nature of the image, and its formation. Some scientists were even prepared to suggest that the image had been somehow 'burned' on to the cloth, by a burst of radiation energy released during Christ's resurrection. There seemed little left but admiration and awe in the presence of so numinous an object.

What is the Shroud?

The impressive and beautiful face on the Shroud has always been an important factor in persuading people that the Man on the Shroud is indeed Jesus. There are numbers of ancient traditions which tell that Jesus left his facial image imprinted on cloth, images 'not-made-by-hands', which were treasured and venerated and copied, thus becoming the prototypes of the standard images of Christ familiar from centuries of Christian art. That such traditional images and their derivatives conform to the Shroud face had been noted by Vignon, and his iconographic conclusions were substantially augmented in 1978, when Dr Alan Whanger devised a technique for overlaying the Shroud image with images from ancient icons of Jesus. In many instances, he was able to show up to 170 points of similarity between the images; thereby demonstrating to his satisfaction that the face was actually the original from which the iconic type was derived. This is an important point, given the known history of the Shroud.

At one time there were numbers of *acheiropoietos*, or 'not-made-by-hands', images of Christ's face to be found throughout Christendom, such as the Mandylion of Edessa and the Veil of Veronica, and these are known from a multitude of copies. Some of them, it is claimed, survive even today, and research shows that this whole group of images corresponds in striking detail to the face on the Shroud. It is surprising, then, to learn that the majority of these alternative portraits of Christ, all of which can be shown to be the works of human artists, have a demonstrable history far older than that of the Shroud. For the Turin Shroud is first recorded in the fourteenth century.

The Shroud in History

In 1353 the knight Geoffrey de Charny founded a collegiate church at Lirey, in France. In 1356 he

was killed fighting the English at the battle of Poitiers, and the Shroud is heard of for the first time in the following year, when his widow Jeanne exhibited it to pilgrims. Where it came from, or how it came into the keeping of the de Charnys, is nowhere so much as hinted at. Modern researchers have tried to provide a provenance for it. The most coherent attempt is that of Ian Wilson, the British author of a number of books on the Shroud, who suggested that it should be identified with the Edessa Mandylion, traceable to the sixth century, which was transferred to the imperial relic hoard in Constantinople in 944. There a cloth which appears to have looked rather like the Shroud, and which was described as 'the sydoine in which our Lord had been wrapped', was seen by the Frenchman Robert de Clari in 1203. Wilson postulated that the Mandylion/sydoine/Shroud was looted from Constantinople in 1204, and eventually brought to France by the Templars, one of whom, Geoffrey de Charny, may have been related to the Lirey de Charnys. The story is ingenious rather than convincing, but that the relic came from Constantinople is plausible enough.

Its subsequent history is well documented. In 1418 the Lirey canons placed the Shroud for safekeeping with Jeanne and Geoffrey's granddaughter Margaret, who in 1453 gave it to Duke Louis of Savoy. The House of Savoy eventually placed the cloth in the so-called Sainte-Chapelle, their family chapel in Chambéry, which was restored and beautified as a fitting shrine for the Shroud.

Today, the most obvious thing seen on the Shroud is not the pale image, but two rows of patches, stains and scorches, which run the entire length of the cloth on either side of the figure. These result from an accident that almost destroyed the mysterious secret of the Shroud centuries before it was revealed. On 4 December 1532 fire broke out in the Sainte-Chapelle, and by the time the Shroud was rescued its silver reliquary had begun to melt. Molten drops of metal dripped along one edge of the folded cloth, burning right through the entire relic. Two years later nuns patched the linen and the expositions began again.

The Shroud was the most prized possession of the House of Savoy, and when they moved their capital to Turin, it was inevitable that it should move with them, in 1578. It remained in the

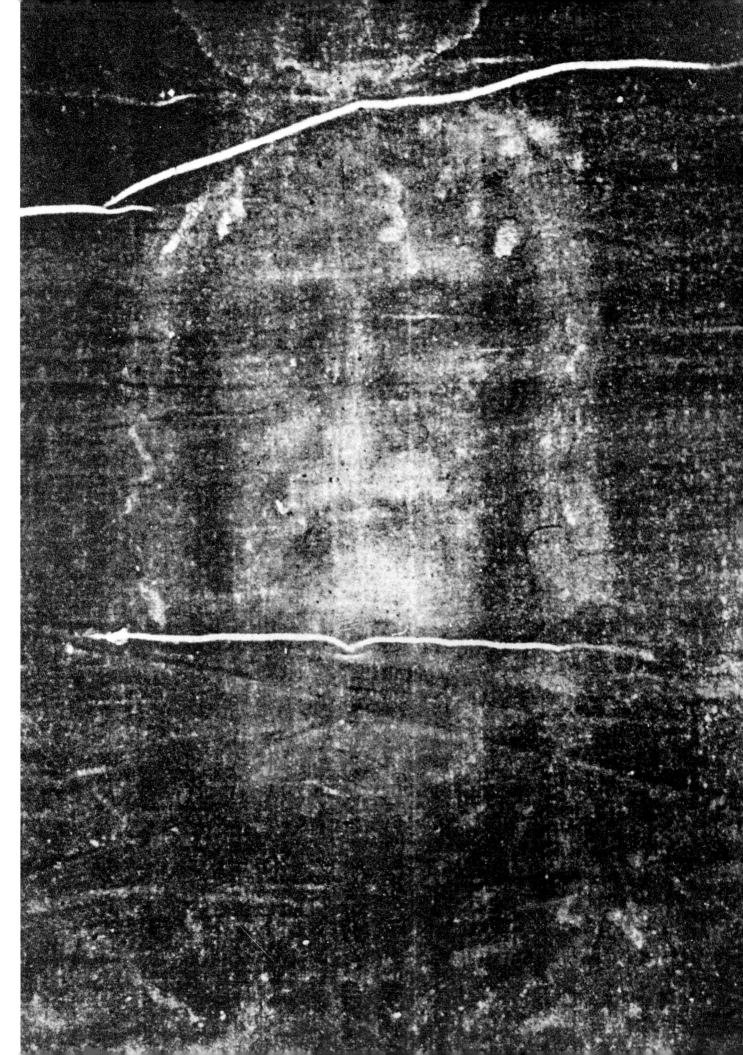

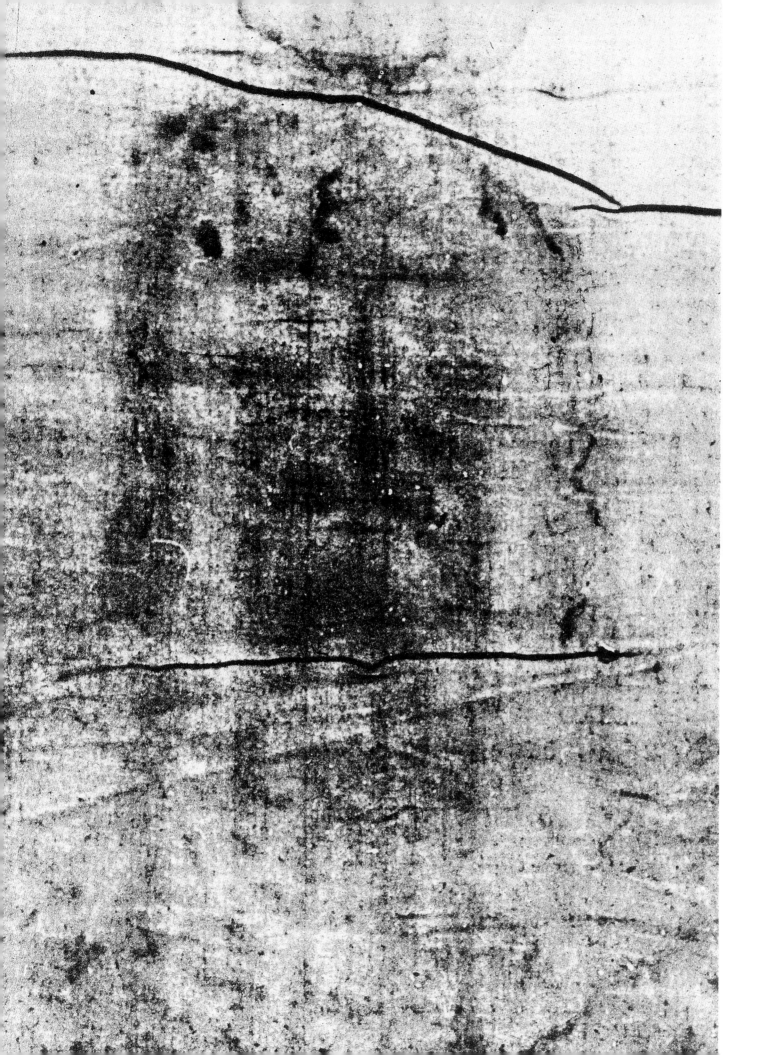

palace chapel, the focus of ever-increasing devotion, until 1694, when it was transferred to a sumptuous purpose-built Baroque chapel in the cathedral. Here it has remained ever since. The Shroud remained the property of the Savoy royal family until 1983, when ex-King Umberto II bequeathed it to the pope on his deathbed.

Though increasingly the Shroud came to be seen as evidently self-vindicating, the Church itself has never pronounced on it, preferring to see it as a magnificent religious image rather than as a relic. Immediately after the first exposition in 1357, Henri of Poitiers, Bishop of Troyes, is said to have forbidden further exhibitions, and when, in 1389, the de Charnys obtained papal permission to show the Shroud again, another bishop of Troyes, Pierre d'Arcis, twice wrote to Clement VII to protest. His principal objection, d'Arcis said, was based on a memorandum of Henri of Poitiers, revealing that the Lirey clergy had, 'falsely and deceitfully', obtained 'a certain cloth, cunningly painted, upon which by a clever sleight of hand was depicted the twofold image of one man . . . pretending that this was the actual shroud in which our Saviour Jesus Christ was enfolded' – a fact 'attested by the artist who had painted it'.

This damning evidence has been freely used by opponents of the Shroud, seeking to brand it a forgery. In the Middle Ages the forging of religious relics was not unknown; research has shown that some thirty-five shrouds of Christ were claimed in various places, at various times. Some were plain lengths of linen; others, such as the Shroud of Besançon, bore images not dissimilar to that on the Turin Shroud. Most of these, however, including the Besançon example, can be shown to be painted copies of the Turin cloth.

Against this evidence it may be noted that although the actual autograph of d'Arcis's letter has survived, the claimed memorandum of Henri of Poitiers has not, and might well itself have been a forgery by a powerful ecclesiastic resentful of someone going over his head to petition papal permission for the expositions. Although much has been made of Clement's blood-relationship with the de Charnys, it seems unlikely that the pope would have been able to suppress d'Arcis's opposition so thoroughly had the memorandum been genuine. Had it existed, others would have seen it.

Similarly, it is possible that the numerous copies of Besançon and elsewhere argue for the primacy – if not the authenticity – of the Turin Shroud.

Last is the argument from art. The Shroud is documented since 1357, yet no truly comparable medieval images exist. No one has yet explained satisfactorily how anyone, let alone a medieval forger, could have programmed so many hidden data into the relic; nor have they satisfactorily suggested why, even if they could, anyone should have encoded information which no one would be able to access for more than five centuries.

Though brushed aside by Clement VII, Bishop d'Arcis's claim has in recent years been taken as fact by those wishing to set aside the findings of STURP and other pro-Shroud researchers. For some years, the memorandum's most persistent advocate has been US microbiologist Walter McCrone, who had earlier exposed the so-called Vinland Map as a modern forgery. Never having seen the Shroud for himself, McCrone was given access to debris collected from the Shroud surface by the STURP team, which he quickly pronounced to be the remains of medieval artists' pigments. STURP's own findings were that the image was naturally formed, and that the pigmentation found scattered over the Shroud's surface was incidental, and not directly related to the image. Without in any way doubting Dr McCrone's professionalism, cause for concern for his objectivity might be found in a revealing statement made by him to an American journalist in 1980: 'The Shroud is a fake, but I cannot prove it'. As with other contemporary detractors, one has the impression that McCrone had long ago made up his mind that the Shroud was a 'fake', and sought evidence to buttress his belief, rather than assessing the actual evidence.

The Evidence of Carbon-dating

At this period opinion hardened on both sides. Demands were increasingly heard for the cloth to undergo what was seen by many as the ultimate and definitive test, the dating of the cloth by measuring its carbon-14 content. Tiny amounts of the radioactive isotope carbon-14 are absorbed by all living things, and over time this decays at a fixed rate; calculating the rate of decay of the carbon-14 in an object theoretically permits the approximate

The shrine of the Holy Shroud in Turin Cathedral.

time in history in which the object was alive to be fixed. Popularly, the accuracy of radiocarbon dating was held to be more or less absolute, and supporters and detractors of the Shroud alike

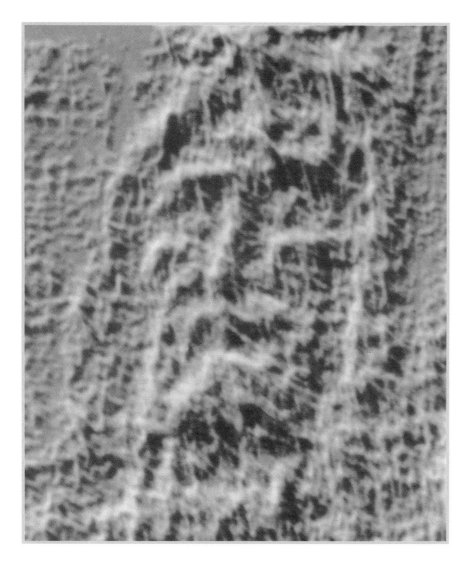

The Shroud image yields up another secret to modern science: 3-D information is encoded in the negative image.

believed that the test would settle the argument once and for all.

The Church finally agreed to the test. In April 1988 tiny samples of the cloth were taken, and forwarded to laboratories in Tucson, Arizona, in Oxford, and in Zurich, in Switzerland. With the Shroud samples went fragments of other ancient fabrics, whose ages were already known, to act as controls. The tests were co-ordinated by Dr Michael Tite of the British Museum. By the autumn all three laboratories had completed their work, and on 14 October the result was

announced simultaneously in Turin, by Cardinal Ballestero, for the Church, and in London, by Dr Tite, for the three laboratories. The flax from which the linen of the Shroud had been woven had been harvested some time between 1260 and 1390. Around the world, the Turin Shroud was denounced as a 'forgery' by the media.

Almost immediately these tests, which should have settled the matter, themselves became a matter of controversy. The results had been leaked weeks before 14 October and persons not authorized to participate at the testings had been admitted: in both instances breaking the protocol agreed to beforehand. Far from it having been a blind testing, Dr Paul Damon of Tucson admitted that the distinctive weave of the Shroud had made it easy to recognize. For many, the most disturbing aspect of the whole thing was perhaps the glee with which certain scientists publicly exulted over the downfall of the Shroud. As Professor Hall of the Oxford laboratory told the press on 14 October, 'There was a multi-million-pound business in making forgeries during the fourteenth century. Someone just got a bit of linen, faked it up, and flogged it.' No mention of the unique and inexplicable nature of the image, which has never been reproduced satisfactorily. If nothing else, this contemptuous, and contemptible, statement demonstrates how thoroughly certain upholders of a rigid scientific orthodoxy had been rattled by the mystery of the Shroud.

In fact, it rapidly became clear that, apart from the scientists directly involved, almost no one was satisfied with the tests. Many believers found that the results did not disturb their belief, and said so; others felt that the tests themselves were faulty or improperly conducted (though there is no evidence to substantiate this), and wanted a re-testing — especially after it became widely known that all the radiocarbon dates published with the authority of the British Museum between 1980 and 1984 had been incorrect.

A Mystery Unresolved

Far from disappearing instantly from view, as its opponents had hoped, its mystery neatly eliminated by science, the Shroud continues to intrigue and baffle, and new studies continue to appear regularly. The evident failure of the scientific community to provide a sustainable explanation has meant that much of this new work is speculative and often simply bizarre. The German writers Holger Kersten and Elmar Gruber, for example, have tried to prove that the carbon-14 tests were 'fixed' by the Vatican, anxious to discredit the relic, but as the rest of their book is an attempt to show that Jesus survived the crucifixion and moved to India, and as, for evidence of this, they need the Shroud to be genuine, their conspiracy-theory plea is easily understandable – while their evidence for this is not. Even weirder is the recent claim by Lynn Picknett and Clive Prince that the Shroud was forged by Leonardo da Vinci, who, having invented photography and joined the Priory of Sion, placed his own face on the cloth deliberately to subvert Christianity when eventually the truth was discovered in the future, as Leonardo foresaw it would be. This theory, ignoring equally the carbon-dating to well before da Vinci's birth and the image already witnessed to by d'Arcis in 1389, has been aptly compared by the writer Stuart Gordon not only to flogging a dead horse, but attempting to ride it at the same time.

Fortunately other researchers have a clearer grasp of the plausible, and the most rewarding research at present concerns itself with the actual nature of the image on the cloth. Although numbers of researchers are prepared to accept the carbon-14 dating, and are attempting to demonstrate how it was made in the fourteenth century, others again see the image as containing its own proof of authenticity. Even at the time when the test results were being leaked in 1988, the English expert on medieval painting Anna Hulbert said that the idea that the Shroud could be dated only from the fourteenth century raised 'more problems [for] an art historian than if it [was] genuinely the Shroud of Jesus'. If one accepts that, for whatever reason, the radiocarbon dating was suspect and that substantial support for the Shroud's genuineness is derived from all the other evidence, then the words of the archaeologist Dr Eugenia Nitowski to Ian Wilson should be considered:

In any form of enquiry or scientific discipline, it is the weight of evidence which must be considered conclusive. In archaeology, if there are ten lines of evidence, carbon dating being one of them, and it

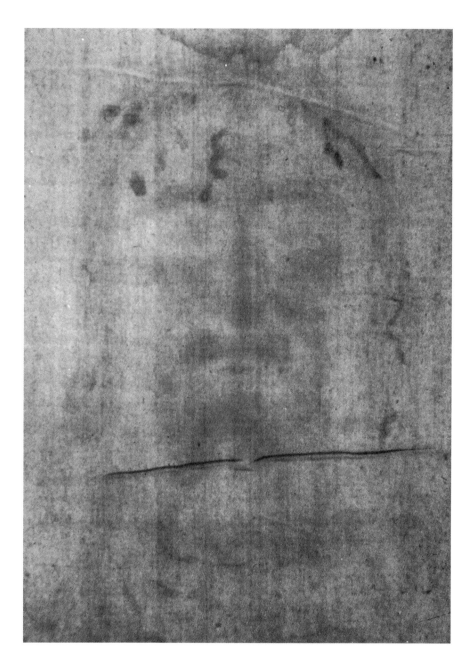

conflicts with the other nine, there is little hesitation to throw out the carbon date as inaccurate.

The Man in the Shroud – the real face of Jesus?

Which leaves us – with what? With a deepening mystery. Far from being solved, for most open-minded people, the jury is still out on the Holy Shroud of Turin, and is likely to remain so for some considerable time to come.

THE
HOLY GRAIL

CHRISTOPHER KNIGHT
& ROBERT LOMAS

Legends come and go but the story of the Holy Grail has endured in western folklore ever since the middle of the twelfth century. Today the phrase 'seeking the Holy Grail' means any search for definitive knowledge, and has a connotation of something as illusory and futile as hunting for the pot of gold at the end of a rainbow.

The Power of the Holy Grail

The most common definition of the Holy Grail is that it was the sacred cup from which Jesus Christ drank at the Last Supper. According to common legend this precious cup was kept by a man who gave up his own tomb so that Jesus could be buried in a way befitting the Messiah. This man was Joseph of Arimathea, who is said to have used the holy cup to collect the blood that flowed from Christ's wounds as he was nailed to the cross. Many years later Joseph left Jerusalem with the Grail to travel to Glastonbury in Britain where he arrived in AD 73. From that time onwards, it is said, the Grail has been secretly transmitted from generation to generation of Joseph's descendants in the British Isles.

There have also been other variations of the legend of the Holy Grail which describe it not as any kind of cup, but as 'the stone upon which kings

are made' or even as 'a book that contains the secret teachings of Jesus'.

Most people today assume that the Holy Grail is purely mythical, and yet many serious-minded researchers have found cause to investigate the possibility of it being a real artefact. Until relatively recently we would have sided fully with the sceptics, considering it no more than a medieval Christian myth. But in 1995, whilst researching something quite different we stumbled upon new evidence that changed our view completely.

One does not have to believe in magic or mira-

cles to have an interest in the Holy Grail because there is real history as well as myth to consider. It is widely accepted that Jesus Christ was once a living person and, as he has been hailed as the Son of God from his own time to this, it is not unreasonable to assume that his followers could have preserved this ceremonial drinking cup. Had they done so it would certainly have been venerated and viewed as the greatest treasure in the whole of Christendom.

If the Holy Grail was preserved after the crucifixion of Jesus it must have been kept very secret

for the first 1,100 hundred years, because the very first written reference did not appear until around 1140. The story of the Holy Grail was quickly connected to the mythical story of King Arthur, which had been introduced just a few years earlier.

The popular versions of the Arthurian legend and the Grail that we all see in films and on television today are mainly based on the later romantic works of Sir Thomas Mallory, written in the fifteenth century. In these tales the Grail is said to possess many miraculous properties, such as the power of furnishing food for those without sin, of

Glastonbury Tor, where Joseph of Arimathea was reputed to have planted his staff as the Holy Thorn tree.

159

King Arthur shown in a twelfth-century mosaic.

blinding the impure of heart or striking dumb the irreverent who come into its presence.

Great legends develop and are sustained because they hold values that people admire and the delicate line between fact and fiction often becomes blurred. With most of these folk tales it is impossible to identify where and when they started, but the story of the Grail is unusual because it has a definite starting point. The first the world knew of such an artefact was from the pen of an ageing monk and historian who lived in Malmesbury Abbey, between Oxford and Bristol. William of Malmesbury composed his saga of Joseph of Arimathea shortly after a nearby cleric called Geof-

frey of Monmouth had published the first story of King Arthur in his book *The Matter of Britain*.

The two ecclesiastical neighbours both claimed to know the truth and each accused the other of telling false accounts of King Arthur. From the very first references the Holy Grail was described as having been lost at some earlier date, and the task for all concerned was to recover the missing treasure.

Geoffrey of Monmouth claimed that his story was historically accurate and that he had found the details recorded in an old document that had been brought to his attention. His story depicted King Arthur as a supernatural saviour of his people with a kingdom at Caerleon, beginning in the year AD

The Knights of the Round Table with the Grail, from a fourteenth-century French drawing.

505 and ending when the King was carried westwards to the sacred isle of Avalon, where he rests until a time of great need when he will return again.

When these stories first appeared they quickly spread across the whole of Europe and for several centuries were considered to be historical fact.

Just at the time that these fabulous stories were becoming popular a new order of knights was making a name for itself and many people considered them to be as magical and inspiring as the Knights of the Round Table. The Knights Templar were a strange order of crusader monks based in Jerusalem, who were said to have found the Holy Grail and to have become its secret guardians. The Templars adopted white tunics with a large red cross and they grew shoulder-length hair and beards in the style of first-century priests of Jerusalem. Their dress has now become synonymous with the image of a crusader.

Within months of their establishment in 1128 they became fabulously rich and rumours spread that they conducted strange initiation ceremonies in secret.

The Treasures of Jerusalem

To understand how the Knights Templar could have been connected with a relic that they believed was the Holy Grail we must now return to first-

161

century Jerusalem to find the possible root of the legend of the Holy Grail.

As we, and other researchers have found, the stories told in the New Testament are not a very accurate rendering of events. Many leading churchmen will now admit that many of the stories told in the Gospels are largely myth, conveying the spirit of Christianity rather than its history. The Jerusalem Church believed that there was a need for two messiahs; one to be king and one to be high priest. These messiahs were not viewed as gods but as earthly leaders who would create a kingdom fit for their God, Yahweh, to rule over. At the very centre of the Jewish faith was the Temple at Jerusalem, built by Solomon and rebuilt by King Herod during the lifetime of Jesus and his brother James.

At the eastern entrance of the Jerusalem Temple stood two pillars called Boaz and Jachin, which were believed to represent the power of the two messiahs – one of a kingly line, descended from David, and one of a priestly line, descended from Aaron, the priestly brother of Moses.

After Jesus was crucified he was succeeded by his brother James, who was himself murdered in AD 62. Possibly because of the killing of James, the Jews started a terrible war that eventually led to the destruction of them and their Temple.

The strange truth is that by the time the authors of the Gospels of Matthew, Mark, Luke and John first put pen to paper everyone who had known Jesus and his followers was dead, along with most of the population of Israel. Although the Bible does not mention it, we know from a man called Josephus, who was an eye-witness to the destruction of Jerusalem, that over 1.3 million Jewish men women and children died by the sword between AD 66 and 73.

The most devout Jews, including the group we now call the Jerusalem Church, had acquired the great wealth of the city and it is now known that they believed that they were instructed by God to bury their most precious artefacts beneath the Temple in Jerusalem, as close as they could get to

the 'Holy of Holies' – the inner chamber where God Himself was present.

In 1946 a cache of scrolls was found hidden in a desert location south-east of Jerusalem, which had been the site of the religious Jewish community of Qumran 2,000 years ago. Among these famous documents, known to us as the Dead Sea Scrolls, was a very important list, written on copper, which records how the Jews buried their treasure underneath the Temple before the Romans made their final assault. This Copper Scroll identifies exactly where different treasures and scrolls were buried and it lists bars of gold, hundreds of pitchers of silver coins, scrolls and many cups and other vessels; fabulous riches by any standards.

This Copper Scroll was written just before the fall of the Temple and the twelfth entry, typical of the sixty-one entries, says:

In the Court of [unreadable word], nine cubits under the southern corner: gold and silver vessels for tithe, sprinkling basins, cups, sacrificial bowls, libation vessels, in all six hundred and nine.

These artefacts were buried by a group which included many people who had known Jesus personally. If a cup or sacrificial blood-collecting bowl associated with Jesus existed, it would have been buried here with the treasures of the Jews.

These Jewish resistance fighters buried their precious objects in the spring of AD 68, and the Dead Sea Scrolls were hidden in the caves around Qumran shortly afterwards. They acted just in time, because Roman forces destroyed

Josephus, son of Joseph of Arimathea, shown with the Grail; from the fourteenth-century French Queste de Saint-Graal.

163

Qumran only weeks later, in the month of June. Two years later the holy Temple of the Jews lay in ruins and the members of the Jerusalem Church had been slain by the Romans. All memory of the secret horde was lost. The Holy Grail and everything precious to the people that knew Jesus Christ was buried under thousands of tons of tumbled masonry.

The Kings of God

The priests of the Temple of Jerusalem preserved the genealogies of the lines of David and Aaron and the Bible tells us that Jesus was descended from David on Joseph's side and from Aaron on Mary's side, making him a possible messiah for both lines. Our own recent research has indicated that when the Romans destroyed the Temple in AD 70, some of the hereditary priests of the Temple managed to escape to Europe in order to preserve their 1,000-year-old bloodlines.

It is very interesting to note that legend says that Joseph of Arimathea brought the Holy Grail to Britain in AD 73; just three years after the fall of the Temple. This is significant because the originators of the Grail stories were Christians and it is unlikely that they would have realized the importance of this date because the New Testament does not record the fall of the Jerusalem Temple.

While the date fits well, there is a problem with the idea that Joseph of Arimathea travelled to Britain in AD 73 and then continued his bloodline. The difficulty is that we are told in the Bible that Joseph allowed Jesus to be buried in the tomb that he had prepared for himself. Jesus had died around forty years before, so Joseph must have been a very young man at the time of the Crucifixion; and young men do not usually spend money preparing their own graves.

It seems probable that the people who arrived in Britain were the children or even grandchildren of Joseph of Arimathea and it is his bloodline that was important. We also have good reason to believe that these descendants of the hereditary priests of the Temple did not have the Holy Grail with them. It was already lost . . . but they knew where it rested – under the ruins of Herod's Temple.

Over the following centuries the descendants of the surviving high priests of the Temple founded some of the leading families of Europe and they

secretly transmitted the story of the lost Holy Grail down the generations for the next 1,000 years.

By the end of the eleventh century these families were fully Christianized on the surface, but secretly they knew the location of the Holy Grail and all of the great treasures of their Jewish ancestors. These families with ancient Jewish bloodlines called themselves 'Rex Deus', which is Latin for 'the kings of God' – but only a chosen son of each generation was told the full secrets of their past and the story of the treasures buried under the Temple.

These families included the Counts of Champagne, the Counts of Anjou, the St Clairs, the Counts of Fountain and the de Bouillon family, and in 1071 something happened that caused these families to return to Jerusalem. That year the city was devastated by Seljuk Turks which the Rex

PAPA HONORIVS

Deus families saw as the fulfilment of a prophecy written in the Book of Revelations that said Jerusalem would be attacked by heathens led by Gog and Magog, 1,000 years after the fall of the city in AD 70. In chapter twenty the visionary author describes how the resurrected martyrs who had died defending Jerusalem from the Romans, would return at this time.

The Turks had taken the city exactly 1,000 years later and the Rex Deus families saw themselves as the 'resurrected' bloodline who would return to free Jerusalem. They used their considerable influence to raise the greatest army that Europe had ever seen, and on 15 July 1099 these crusaders captured Jerusalem. Then, with an efficiency not seen since Roman times, they massacred every man, woman and child in the name of God.

The Rex Deus families then turned their attention to establishing the strange order of the Knights Templar who were both priests and warriors. They knew of the treasures that lay beneath the ruins of the Temple of Jerusalem from the stories that had been handed down from father to son for 1,000 years, and in 1118 they started excavating below the ruined Temple.

Amongst the wonderful treasures that they found was a particularly precious vessel, and whilst many items must have been melted down, this special cup was kept and revered as the Holy Grail itself.

Hugh de Payens, the first Grand Master of the Templars, visited Scotland, where his old friend and uncle by marriage, Henri St Clair lived. Henri had been one of the Rex Deus members who captured Jerusalem and on his return to Scotland he

Hugh de Payens being invested as the first Grand Master of the Knights Templar by Pope Honorius.

had been made a baron. He must have been very excited that the Rex Deus families had used their ancient knowledge to retake Jerusalem exactly as prophesied, and he celebrated the occasion by taking a very unusual title for himself. He called himself the 'Baron of Roslin'. In Scottish Gaelic the short word Roslin has the very significant meaning, 'ancient knowledge passed down the generations'. In 1140 the Templars moved the

scrolls and treasures, including the Holy Grail, to lands owned by the St Clair family in Kilwinning, where they built an abbey.

It can be no coincidence that the stories of the Holy Grail and King Arthur suddenly appeared in the twelve years between the finding of the treasures below the Temple and their arrival in Kilwinning. Both of the early creators of the Arthurian and Grail stories had direct contact with Payen de Montdidier, one of the founding Knights Templars when he lived in England.

The stories of Arthur, the Grail Quest and the Templars as guardians of the Grail were soon developed by such medieval writers as Chretien de Troyes and Wolfram von Eschenbach, and later by Thomas Mallory.

The ground plan of Roslin Chapel, built 1440, is identical with that of Herod's Temple. This couldn't be an accident.

Plan of Roslin showing how the Triple Tau and the Seal of Solomon formed the design theme of the whole building.

Roslin Chapel, Midlothian, built by Sir William St Clair to house the secrets of the Templars.

The Grail Sanctuary at Roslin

The Templars kept their rituals secret for almost 200 years, until on Friday 13 October 1307 they were arrested as heretics and soon destroyed as an order. The St Clair family still held the scrolls and some of the treasures from Jerusalem. The question is, did they still have the Holy Grail?

We think the answer is yes, because in 1440 Sir William St Clair decided to build a very strange building which survives to this day. It is a small stone building that has been mistakenly identified as a chapel. Every inch both inside and out is carved with strange symbols, but the strangest feature of all is that below ground the building is an exact replica of the ground-plan of ruins of the Temple at Jerusalem that the Knights Templars excavated. To the west is a replica of the ruined west wall of the Temple, which still stands in Jerusalem, but above ground the building is like a book carved in stone; but a book that is written in a language that is difficult for us to read.

Sir William St Clair of Roslin left clues by adding words to the verbal rituals that had come from the Templars and are still used by Freemasons. In the east are two magnificent pillars, just where they would have been in the Jerusalem Temple, but the other pillars of the building form a symbol called a Triple Tau (referring to the Greek letter of that name). William St Clair tells us through the rituals of Freemasonry that this ancient Jewish symbolic layout has the following mysterious meaning: 'The Temple of Jerusalem, a key to a treasure, a place where a precious thing is concealed, and the precious thing itself.'

This building at Roslin in Scotland has never been excavated so whatever Sir William inherited from the Templars has not been disturbed. Whatever ancient knowledge had been passed down the generations he made safe beneath this reconstruction of Herod's Temple and it is almost certain that it is still there. One day soon modern archaeology may be able to once again recover the lost Holy Grail and the secret teachings of Jesus that lie buried with it.

167

THE **KNIGHTS TEMPLAR**

NICHOLAS BEST

On a March day in 1314, after seven years of torture and imprisonment, two old men were dragged in chains through the streets of Paris. Followed by a jeering crowd, they were hustled towards one of the islands in the Seine. There they were stripped to their underwear before being tied to a stake set up close to the great cathedral of Notre Dame.

King Philip watches as Geoffrey de Charney and Jacques de Molay are burned at the stake.

The Templars' Curse

The men were Geoffrey de Charney and Jacques de Molay. They were respectively the Preceptor of Normandy and the Grand Master of the Order of the Knights Templar. They were about to burn to death for a host of alleged crimes – including sacrilege, blasphemy, sodomy, Devil worship and the practice of Black Magic.

But there was still time to repent. Even as the firewood was heaped around them, the two men were given every chance to confess their sins. If they confessed, they would not have to die. They would be taken back to prison instead, back to a slower, more lingering punishment in solitary con-

finement, left to rot in the dark with their legs in irons and no prospect of ever being released. Other Templars had chosen solitary confinement instead of death. De Charney and de Molay could too, if they wished.

Both men refused. They would not admit to worshipping the Devil. They protested their innocence instead, renouncing confessions they had made earlier under torture, insisting that they had always been innocent in the eyes of God. They were prepared to die now, if that was His will, rather than admit to the charges against them.

A final attempt was made to dissuade them. Red hot coals were shovelled around them, slowly roast-ing them alive. There was still a chance to change their minds, still an opportunity to save themselves from the fire.

The men were adamant. The Grand Master asked that his hands should not be tied, so that he could die in prayer. He asked that his body should be turned on the stake, that he might see Notre Dame one last time before the end. His wishes were granted and the fire was lit. The two men observed it without flinching. They were calm and composed, perfectly prepared to meet their Maker.

Gradually the fire took hold. As the flames rose, the Grand Master raised his eyes to Heaven and uttered a curse. It was a loud curse, resonant, full

The cathedral of Notre Dame in Paris, scene of the execution of de Charney and de Molay.

169

of anguish; a curse heard not only by the spectators on the island but by all of France, a curse that echoed down the centuries and was remembered by Frenchmen everywhere, even as late as the French Revolution. It was a curse on the enemies of the Templars – on the Pope who had condemned the Order, on King Philip of France who had persecuted its members, on everyone who had ever opposed the Knights Templar, whoever they might be: 'Let evil overcome those who have condemned us!' the Grand Master swore. 'God will avenge our death. God will grant justice. Let our enemies suffer, as we have suffered, for what they have done!'

The crowd shrank from the Grand Master's words. Even as they did though, the flames were gathering pace. The Grand Master's voice cracked and died, was heard no more. His body began to bubble and blacken, his flesh melting from his bones as it disintegrated in the fierce heat. The Preceptor's flesh melted too. Before long, nothing was left of either of them except a few charred bones and a heap of ash still too hot to touch. The two men were dead. With them, for all practical purposes, had died the 200-year-old Order of Knights Templar.

That night, after the fire had cooled and the crowd had dispersed, a group of sympathizers stole across to the island and quietly retrieved the bones of the two martyrs for proper burial elsewhere.

Thirty-three days later the Pope died. A few months after that, King Philip too lay dead and France was plunged into anarchy and chaos for the next 100 years. The curse of the Grand Master had been amply fulfilled.

Who were the Templars?

What kind of people were these Templars? Were they the simple warrior monks they professed to be? Or were they the Devil worshippers of legend, the mysterious idolaters and sorcerers who roasted their own children, performed secret midnight rituals with animals and were guilty of every kind of sexual malpractice? Which of these versions is true?

Their origins were simple enough. They were fighting men, Frankish knights who had fought in the First Crusade and accompanied the victorious army to Jerusalem. There they had banded together in 1118 to form an order of warrior

monks, pledged to protect the lives of pilgrims travelling to the holy places.

There were only nine Templars to begin with, led by Hugh de Payens and Geoffrey of St Omer. They were all devout, all committed to poverty, chastity and obedience. From the first, though, they differed from other religious orders in that they were specifically military in character, a body of fighting men wholly dedicated to the defence of the Christian faith. They differed also from military organizations in their poverty and humility, always wearing shabby clothes instead of the traditional finery expected of warrior knights.

At first, there was nowhere to house this unique Order, but accommodation was soon found beside the Dome of the Rock and the western wall, two of Jerusalem's most sacred places. The accommodation was built on the supposed site of the Temple of Solomon. It was from this that the Knights Templar got their name.

They prospered at once, for there were no regular troops in the Holy Land. The crusader armies had gone home after Jerusalem was captured, leaving only a motley garrison to defend the holy places against Muslim attack. The Knights Templar offered to fill this gap. Their offer was accepted with alacrity.

They needed money to help them, because defence of the Holy Land did not come cheap. There were castles to be built, strong-points, barracks for the troops. Accordingly, money was raised from every country in Christendom – so much in fact that although Templars personally were never well off, their Order eventually became enormously rich, far richer than it needed to be for its original intended purpose.

Nevertheless, the Templars provided value for money – at first, anyway. They fought hard throughout all the subsequent crusades and could always be counted on when they were needed. That their efforts met with only mixed success was hardly their fault, for the Christians in the Holy Land found themselves against increasingly stiff opposition as time wore on – not least from the Muslim forces led by Saladin, ruler of Egypt. After many years of struggle, he finally captured Jerusalem in 1187. The Templars were ousted from their original home and forced to decamp. They remained in the Holy Land until 1303, but

they were never again to set foot in Jerusalem, the city they had sworn to defend with their lives.

By then however, the Order had changed considerably in character. What had begun as a simple body of fighting men was now far more complex and sinister. After many years of handling the finances needed for the crusades (the cash was kept safe in Templar castles), they had become bankers and money-men as well as soldiers – the most sophisticated bankers in all of Europe. They had become property owners, owning 9,000 manors in many different lands. They had become religious

After capturing Jerusalem in 1099, the crusaders killed thousands of Muslims before looting the city.

171

Krak de Chevaliers at Homs, in Syria, a crusader stronghold.

dignitaries, enjoying special immunities granted to them by the Pope. Yet they remained still a law unto themselves, a mysterious society swearing allegiance always to each other, rather than to any king or country: a society with no apparent reason for existence after its expulsion from the Holy Land.

The Persecution of the Templars

This was obviously a recipe for disaster. A rich and secret society, powerful, arrogant, forbidden to women, yet meeting only behind closed doors and accountable to no one but itself. It was inevitable that jealousies should arise about the Templars, that rumours should begin to spread. And spread they eventually did, all across Europe.

How far the rumours were true, and how far they were merely a trumped-up excuse to seize the Templars' vast wealth, is impossible to say at this distance. What is certain though is that the rumours were lurid in the extreme, varying from heresy and witchcraft to kissing the anus of a black cat and sleeping with the Devil in the guise of a

172

beautiful woman. There was talk of mysterious initiation ceremonies in which men kissed each other on the lips, the navel and the buttocks. It was said also that Templars would spit on the Cross and worship the Devil in a darkened room; that the ashes of their dead were given to new Templars to eat; that virgins were made pregnant and their new-born babies roasted over a fire, the fat being used to anoint the Templars' satanic idols. In a superstitious age, these were very serious accusations indeed.

Perhaps the most serious accusation of all was that the Templars had deliberately abandoned the Holy Land to the Muslims, surrendering to their enemies in a pact with the Devil designed to preserve the Templars' own power and wealth. It was certainly true that they had formed alliances with Muslims in the interests of peace and religious tolerance. They were also suspected of worshipping the devil Baphomet in various forms (usually a jewelled skull, a wooden phallus or an androgynous winged idol, part-woman, part-goat). Baphomet

Templar effigies in a London church. The Temple underground stop is named after their Order.

173

was held to be a corruption of the name Mohammed, and Mohammed was considered by Christians to be the Beast of Revelation, distinguished by his mark and the number 666.

But what really undid the Templars was their

Romanticized nineteenth-century portrait of a Templar.

money. They had become seriously rich by the beginning of the fourteenth century: so rich in England, for example, that Templars there were able to make a substantial contribution towards Edward I's wars against France. This naturally did not go down well with the French, in particular King Philip of France. He was an ambitious

monarch, devious and scheming, but desperately short of finance of his own and, in a turbulent reign, had already debased the coinage several times and expelled the Jews from France, confiscating all their property. By 1307, he was again in urgent need of cash. He looked around for a fresh source of finance – and his eye fell on the Templars.

Their spies had warned them that trouble was coming, but the extent of it came as a shock. They were arrested on the morning of Friday 13 October – all 5,000, every Templar in France. The arrests were co-ordinated so that only a handful escaped, perhaps twenty in all. The rest were rounded up and thrown into prison, even the Grand Master and his officials. The Templars were supposed to enjoy immunity from arrest, but their immunity did not help them now. The Pope owed his position to King Philip and did nothing to save them. Neither did anyone else. Even by the standards of the day, it was an infamous act of betrayal.

The ordinary people of France were deeply disturbed by it. These were holy men, not common criminals. Whatever they had done – and not everyone believed they were in league with the Devil – the Templars should not have been treated thus. It was not the way things were supposed to happen.

Philip's fellow monarchs were not impressed either. He wrote to all his neighbouring kings, explaining his action and inviting them to do the same to their own Templars. Few followed his lead; they did not share his view of the Templars' guilt. It was not until the Pope issued a Bull commanding them to abolish the Order that they complied, and then only with considerable reservations.

Philip however remained adamant. Under French law, the Templars were guilty until proved innocent – and the charges against them were vile in the extreme. Sodomy, obscenity, sacrilege: the king saw to it that the allegations received widespread publicity after the Templars' arrest, the full enormity of their excesses exposed for the first time. He obtained confessions too, from the Grand Master among others, confessions under oath to the vilest depravities imaginable. The Grand Master personally admitted to spitting on the Cross, and other diabolical offences. He begged forgiveness, publicly urging his fellow Templars to follow suit while they still had the chance.

The Grand Master had been tortured, of course, as had the others. In Paris alone, thirty-six Templars died of the effects within a few days of their arrest. Some were starved and beaten, their feet burned until only the bones remained. Others were stretched on the rack until their arms and legs popped out of their sockets, or subjected to the strappado – dropped on a rope with their arms tied behind their back, until their shoulders broke under the strain. Few ultimately refused to confess.

Some Templars did refuse however, a brave and resolute minority. Fifty-four of them were burned at the stake one afternoon, in a field outside Paris. Others disappeared into dungeons, never to be seen again. It was seven years before the last of them had been tried and disposed of. The process was supposed to come to a climax with the public confession of the Grand Master and the Preceptor of Normandy at Notre Dame. In the event though, both men used the occasion to retract their confessions, reaffirming their innocence in front of a crowd of thousands. They were put to death at once, and the Order of the Knights Templar was heard no more.

The Legacy of the Templars

But the Templars were not forgotten. Their properties were confiscated, their Order expunged and those who were not killed or imprisoned scattered far and wide. Yet the idea they represented was too powerful to be extinguished altogether. Their Order was resurrected in the eighteenth century and given a new lease of life as part of the clandestine brotherhood of Freemasonry. Knights Templars have continued as Freemasons ever since.

They were almost certainly innocent of the charges levelled against them by King Philip, but it was the sheer enormity of the offences that has lingered in the public mind, rather than the Templars' denials. Guilty or not, the Templars are always remembered for what was alleged about them, rather than for anything they actually did.

Dante, their contemporary, was in no doubt as to where the guilt should lie for the Templars' demise. In his *Divine Comedy*, he took the Pope and King Philip and put them firmly where they belonged for what they had done – in Hell.

The Templars had revenge, of a sort. In 1793, almost five centuries after the Grand Master's curse, Louis XVI was sent to the guillotine in Paris. His death effectively marked the end of the French monarchy, a long line of despots of whom King

Philip had been only one. After Louis had been executed, it is said that a man came forward from the crowd and dabbled his hands in the blood. The man was a Freemason. He was taking revenge for what had happened to his Templar forebears so many centuries before. Justice, at long last, had been done.

Templar chapels were built all over Christendom. This one is at Mücheln, near Wettin, in Germany.